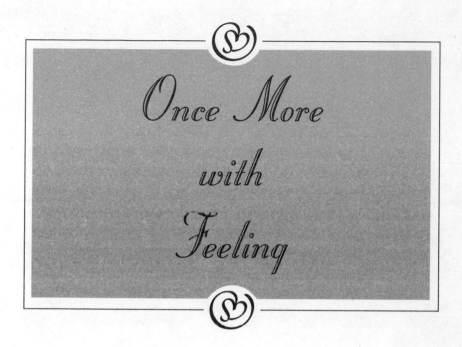

Once More with Feeling

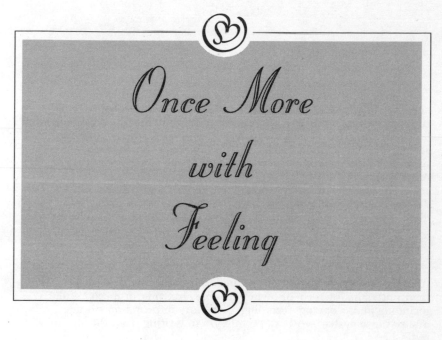

Once More with Feeling

by

MICHELLE, LISA, SOPHIE,
JEWEL, TATIANA, and JENNIFER

as told to

Joanne Parrent
with Bruce W. Cook

DOVE
BOOKS

The publisher of this book has made every effort to insure the accuracy of all material contained in *Once More with Feeling*. Each of the contributors to the book were given polygraph tests by an outside, independent firm to determine the veracity of their stories. All were certified by the examiners as having told the truth. In addition, all of the contributors' accounts were verified by Peter Maheu of Maheu Associates, a private investigation firm, and the manuscript was reviewed twice by attorneys specializing in First Amendment law to determine the validity of legal claims. Although several names and likenesses have been changed, all of the information contained herein is, to the best of the editors' and publisher's knowledge, accurate.

ISBN 0-7871-1035-3

Printed in the United States of America

Dove Books
8955 Beverly Boulevard
Los Angeles, Ca 90048
(310) 786-1600

Distributed by Penguin USA

Text design and layout by Folio Graphics

Portraits of Michelle, Lisa, Sophie, Jewel, and Tatiana
by Rick Penn-Kraus
Photo of Tatiana and Michael Jackson by Kevin Mazur.

First Printing: November 1996

10   9   8   7   6   5   4   3   2   1

Contents

Introduction

Tina Turner, in the title song from her 1984 comeback album, sang poignantly about a woman who was obviously a prostitute, the "Private Dancer" of the title. The song doesn't present prostitution as glamorous, exciting or a lifestyle anyone would want to embrace. In plaintive tones, resigned to her fate, the private dancer of the song just pleases men for money. For her, "any old music will do."

Unfortunately, some readers of the bestselling prequel to this book, *You'll Never Make Love in This Town Again*, felt that the lives of the three highly paid call girls whose stories were recounted in that book were fun and glamorous. Perhaps these readers felt that way because the women in that book were paid more for their services than the prostitute in Tina Turner's song presumably earned. In our society, and particularly in Hollywood, people idealize and romanticize that which is expensive. We are fascinated by the lifestyles of the rich and famous, regardless of whether or not what they do is decadent and disgusting.

When I thought more about the response generated by *You'll Never Make Love in This Town Again*, I realized that men and women often had very different reactions to it. The women I spoke to did not tend to glamorize the lives of those in the book. They either found what they read "very sad" or were angered by it. Many men, seemed to be titillated and amused by the explicit stories it contained. At one point, I was introduced as the writer of the book to a group of men who worked at a local investment banking company. They all laughed or smirked and one red-faced guy with a paunch verbalized what many of them seemed to be thinking. "Ha, ha," he boasted. "I'm a cross between Marcus Allen and James Caan." For those who don't remember these two stories, let's just say that this guy imagined himself to be quite a stud.

Even male celebrities reacted differently to *You'll Never Make Love in This Town Again* than I would have expected. George Hamilton, interviewed on the local news one day shortly after the book came out, said he was upset that he wasn't in it—as though being mentioned in that book was some sort of macho badge of honor.

This was very different from the way most women reacted. They repeatedly lashed out at the "sick" men described in the stories and also at the women themselves for "putting up with that shit over and over."

I had to think about why there was such an opposite, apparently gender-based, reaction to these stories of three former prostitutes and an actress/party girl. Years before Anita Hill brought the issue to national attention, I had written a documentary film about sexual harassment and had learned in doing that film how differently men and women feel about sexual harassment. Men, most often the perpetrators of sexual harassment, usually see it as just fun or innocent flirting. Women, usually the victims, experience it as humiliating and a threat to their jobs—not at all fun. In the same way, I realized that men and women also have very different responses to prostitution.

For most women, prostitution illuminates how bad off we really are. It drives home the upsetting fact that many men think of particular women—and by extension, ultimately all women—as nothing more than sex objects. Prostitution, to women who let themselves think about it, is humiliating and degrading to our humanity and dignity. It threatens relationships and makes clear who really has the power in our society. As Kate Millet wrote in *The Prostitution Papers* in 1971, "It is not sex the prostitute is really made to sell; it is degradation." Most women could see the degradation contained in the stories in *You'll Never Make Love in this Town Again*—and it angered, sickened, and saddened them. Many men, unfortunately, could not.

For most men, prostitution is just a kind of "boys will be boys" thing. I don't think most men, or even most women, realize that prostitution degrades men as well. One verse of Tina Turner's "Private Dancer" describes the attitude of the prostitute to the men she sees. The private dancer feels that the guys are all the same. She doesn't look at their faces, ask their names or even "think of them as human." She only thinks about the money she's earning.

In prostitution, as that song beautifully conveys, neither the man nor the woman thinks of the other as human. It is loveless, emotionless sex. It often involves degrading, humiliating, or even painful acts. It is not about two people mutually giving each other pleasure. It is about one person paying to receive pleasure from the other. The pleasure he receives, however, does not seem to come solely from the physical act. The pleasure is also in the symbol of the act—and prostitution is a compelling symbol of the psychological and financial power men have over women in our society.

As the women I worked with on both books told their stories, they tried hard to understand why they did what they did, in hopes that other women would learn from their mistakes. They struggled to make themselves understood so that they would no longer be just faceless "hookers'' or ''whores'' but real-life women—attractive women faced with the dilemma of how to live in a society that values them more for their beauty and their ability to perform sex acts than for their innocence, their intelligence, their warmth, their humor, their ability to love. In short, their humanity.

To stop the dehumanization that prostitution and a culture that encourages prostitution brings about, the first step has thus been to let people see the faces of both the private dancers and their men.

I received a letter which moved me very much from one man, Dennis, who had read *You'll Never Make Love in This Town Again.* When he was younger Dennis had fallen in love with a woman about ten years his senior. After he had dated her for a few months and had started to fall in love with her, she admitted that she was a call girl and an alcoholic. He was shocked and upset—and he broke up with her. They got back together, however, when she promised to stop hooking. He tried to help her stop drinking and found her a job at a bank through friends of his. Unfortunately, after a while, she couldn't resist turning a couple of tricks. Then a couple more. Despite the fact that he loved her, he had to break up with her again. After they were apart for a year or so, he learned that she died in a fatal accident caused by her drunk driving. He wrote to me, ''I lost someone I loved.'' He said he hoped I would pass on his story to encourage young girls to ''get out (of prostitution) when they're young and not when it's too late.''

I hope his story also encourages young men to love the women in their lives as he did, not to buy sex and not to encourage or allow the women they love to sell themselves. Prostitution can only flourish in a culture like ours when both genders participate in it.

Following in the footsteps of Liza, Linda, and Tiffany,

in this new book, Michelle, Lisa, Sophie, and Jewel have chronicled their experiences with prostitution and with drugs. But like the first book, *Once More With Feeling* is not only about prostitution. It is also about Hollywood. It is about how men and women interact in the movie capital of the world. It is about how many powerful men in this industry—which churns out stories and images, telling the whole world how we should all live life—actually view the women in their own lives. It is about a place where film budgets contain slush funds so that male stars can buy drugs and women. It is about a place where one of the highest compliments a woman can get is that she "is one of the smartest cunts in this town"—a comment a male studio executive made about a female producer who was making a movie for his studio. No matter what women achieve in Hollywood, the sexist mentality that permeates the industry determines that we are too often looked at as "cunts" and/or "hookers."

The other day, a screenwriter I know, "Richard," told me about a recent experience he had with a producer on a film he was writing. The producer happens to be "Alan Smithee," one of the few fairly well-known men in this book for whom we were obligated to use a pseudonym rather than his real name. The story about him is one of the most outrageously disgusting stories in this book, so I was very interested in hearing Richard's experience with him. Richard, who is a nice, intelligent, married man, was writing a draft of a script for the studio where Smithee has his deal. Smithee and the director on the project were having some creative differences regarding which direction they each thought the story should go. Smithee invited Richard into his office to talk about the script. A tall, thin mulatto woman, who looked as though she had been poured into her skimpy dress, was in Smithee's office when

Richard arrived. After a minute, she left the room. Smithee then reached for a small box, and Richard thought perhaps he was going to offer him a cigar, all the ridiculous rage among Hollywood types these days. Instead, Smithee walked over to him and said, "If you write the story my way, you can have her," referring to the woman who had just left the room. "Or, you can have any one of these you want," he continued, opening the cigar box and revealing nude pictures of a number of beautiful women. Richard recognized a few of the women—they were fairly well-known actresses.

Not a "player"—the current euphemism around town for a john or a playboy type—Richard turned down the producer's offer and wrote the story the way he thought was best. Now he no longer gets offers for work from that studio, where Smithee has a lot of power. What is unfortunate is that most people aren't shocked when they hear a story like this one. "That's Hollywood," people say. Indeed, it is. The question, however, is why do we let it stay that way? When Clinton campaign advisor Dick Morris was exposed as regularly seeing Sherry Rowlands, a Washington D.C. prostitute, at least President Clinton fired Morris—though it "saddened" the President. In Hollywood, Morris would probably have gotten a bonus in his next contract to help him pay for his extramarital activity.

This book is about six women in Hollywood, some of whose pictures might well have been in Alan Smithee's cigar box. It includes the stories of women who do sell themselves to men like Smithee, and the stories of young women who, before they had the sense not to, got caught up in a life of drugs and prostitution. It also includes the stories of two women—Jennifer Young and Tatiana Thumbtzen—who have tried to make it in Hollywood without selling their bodies. Their stories reveal how difficult it is for a pretty young woman to maintain her dignity and self-respect in Tinseltown.

Through Jennifer and Tatiana's stories, we see how women performers spend years of their lives hoping for that big break, usually unaware that the odds are stacked against them. They get sucked into the power, the glamour, the possibilities. Despite rejections, they keep trying, hopeful that the next audition will be different. They work at "day jobs" to support themselves. They get sexually harassed but don't say anything because they are afraid it might hurt their career. They are tempted to sleep with men they aren't attracted to in the hopes that those men will help them. They get sucked into a fast lane world of partying and drugs and lose focus on their career. Or, they stay focused and get a few opportunities but not that big break. Not yet. They live on crumbs and keep hoping for caviar.

Hollywood ultimately reveals itself in all these stories as a place and a culture in which money is the only thing really valued, a place in which smut, filth and pornographic behavior are accepted as normal and where common decency and respect for women are foreign concepts. It is a closed, male-dominated culture which not only damages the thousands of women who flock here with dreams of riches and stardom but which, through its products—films, television shows, videos, compact discs, and tapes—has incredible influence on the hearts and minds of our entire society. These stories need to be told because everyone who enjoys movies, television, and popular music is exposed to the images created by men in Hollywood. We deserve to know what these men are really like. I applaud the courage of the six women in this book for coming forward. Their stories are a first step in changing the tune that is played over and over in Hollywood. Someday, I hope, as more and more women tell their stories, name names, and refuse to be Hollywood's private dancers, the lyrics we'll hear will be—"Any old music *won't* do anymore."

Joanne Parrent
Los Angeles, California
November, 1996

PART ONE

Love
for
Rent

Once more, a year after Robin, Liza, Linda, and Tiffany shocked Tinseltown by breaking the code of silence in *You'll Never Make Love in This Town Again*, we have the opportunity to peer into the perverse bedrooms of Hollywood—this time through the eyes of two more highly paid call girls, Michelle and Lisa. Once more we will be surprised, shocked, sickened, saddened, and occasionally amused by what we see.

Michelle and Lisa have some things in common, as well as some very interesting differences. Both from middle-class families, Michelle, the pretty WASP, is a doctor's daughter from Northern California. Lisa, the attractive Jewish daughter of a successful businessman, grew up in the San Fernando Valley. They both were good students in high school, though neither finished more than a semester or two of college. Both decided to sell their bodies for similar reasons—to make a lot of money and to avoid having their hearts broken by the kind of men they were meeting and dating in Hollywood.

In other ways, these two tall blondes are quite different and have taken different paths. Lisa developed serious problems with drugs. Michelle doesn't like drugs and has avoided them in her more than decade-long career as a call girl. Michelle got married along the way, but continued to practice her profession without her husband's knowledge. Lisa has had a series of boyfriends while engaged in the call-girl business, but she was always honest with her lovers about what she did for a living.

Both Lisa's and Michelle's stories reveal a great deal about the famous and powerful men who use prostitutes, as well as about the values of the popular culture–creating dream factory, Hollywood. Tinseltown appears in these stories as a place peopled by many individuals—men and women—who value money more than anything else in life. And in the money-obsessed market culture of Hollywood, sex—like expensive, trendy sunglasses to block out the Southern California sun—is a very popular commodity.

Heidi Fleiss once observed that "sex sells." Nowhere, it seems, does it sell in greater variety and at higher prices than in Hollywood. The highest price, however, may be the one ultimately paid by the young women who sell themselves. Only they can tell us what the cost has really been and, in the stories that follow, Michelle and Lisa have opened their hearts to do so.

Michelle

HEIGHT:	*5'9"*
HAIR:	*Ash blond*
EYES:	*Blue*
WEIGHT:	*115*
PROFESSION:	*Call girl/homemaker*
BORN:	*Santa Cruz, California*
HOBBIES:	*Gardening and hiking*
EDUCATION:	*One semester at community college*
FIRST SEXUAL EXPERIENCE:	*At eighteen, with a wealthy older man who moved me to L.A. and made me his mistress*
GOALS & DESIRES:	*To have kids and to run my own business*
SEXUAL FANTASY:	*None left*
DRUGS:	*Don't like drugs; champagne now and then*
HAPPIEST MEMORY:	*My childhood*
WORST EXPERIENCE:	*Getting pissed on by Don Simpson*
SEX PARTNERS:	*Don Simpson, Mikhail Baryshnikov, Don Johnson, Charlie Sheen, Don Henley, Robert Duvall, and more*

Not Your Average Call Girl

I like to think that I'm not the average, run-of-the-mill call girl. There is one thing in particular about my life that is very different from most other women in the business—I've been happily married for the past ten years. My husband definitely does not know what I do. But practicing my profession has not altered my feelings for him. I love him and I love our life together.

I don't fit the typical hooker profile in other ways as well. I come from a pretty normal family. My father is a doctor. My mother is a very intelligent, involved woman who stayed home with her children but was always active in community and charitable affairs. My parents are still married to one another and my relationship with them today is wonderful, though, of course, they also do not know that I am a call girl.

I grew up in Santa Cruz, a small city in Northern California, and went to a community college there for about six months. As a young girl I didn't experience sexual, physical, or emotional abuse, nor was I the wild girl in high school who slept with the entire football team. I always got pretty good grades, but my heart wasn't in school. I wanted to see the world. Also, unlike a lot of women involved in prostitution, I'm not much of a drinker, nor am I into drugs. I have sex for money, not for drugs.

There are exceptions to any stereotype. Each call girl, like every person, is driven by a unique set of needs and motivations. I wouldn't wish the life of a call girl on anyone else, but I do think my life is as unusual as they come.

SANTA CRUZ, 1982

Sugar Daddy Sergio

I was a pretty normal kid in high school. I wasn't a reclusive nerd, nor was I a rah-rah cheerleader type. The cheerleader-jock crowd in school was not for me—I saw them as conformists. I never wanted to be average. Though I dated a lot of high school boys, I did have a reputation in school for going out with older men. I liked older men and felt I could relate to them better.

My first real boyfriend and the first man that I ever slept with was Sergio, a wealthy Antonio Banderas look-alike. Sergio, who was about forty at the time we met, was probably the closest thing to true love that I've ever experienced. I got involved with him when I was not quite eighteen and was still enrolled at Santa Cruz Community College.

We met on the freeway. Sergio, driving a Mercedes-Benz in the lane next to mine, looked over at me and smiled. I wondered why this handsome man was flirting—I had no makeup on and my hair was inelegantly pulled back in a little ponytail, simply to get it out of my face. He must have seen something he liked, however. He rolled down the window and called out his phone number. Amused, I gave him mine. To my surprise, he soon called and asked me out.

In high school I had had many boyfriends and there was always lots of heavy petting, but I didn't go all the way with any of them. Sergio was the first person who really showed me how to make love. We had sex together on our first date. I couldn't have found a better teacher—he was so handsome and worldly, and he taught me how to be sensual, how not to be afraid of my sexuality and my body. The first time I was with him, his penis hurt me as he entered. He stopped and took it more slowly and easily. It wasn't perfect, but that first experience with Sergio was far better than it would have been with one of my less experienced high school boyfriends.

CENTURY CITY, 1982

A Different Life

At the beginning of our relationship, I would fly back and forth between my home in Santa Cruz and Los Angeles to be with Sergio. One day he asked me to move in with him. I was thrilled. I wanted to get out of Santa Cruz and see the world. At that point I hadn't told my parents about Sergio. I didn't think they would approve of my seeing a man twenty years older than me. So I told them that I was moving to Los Angeles to check out UCLA, but that I didn't want to start school right away. I said I would be living with a girlfriend. I had always been a good kid and my parents trusted my judgment without questioning me.

Sergio and I lived in a very elegant high-rise condo in Century City. He really spoiled me. He took me shopping for clothes and jewelry. We traveled to his home in Spain, to Acapulco, and to other destinations where we stayed in the finest hotels and dined at the best restaurants. I was very impressed. Growing up, I was accustomed to a much more modest, middle-class lifestyle. With Sergio I got a taste for luxurious, expensive things. To this day I don't know exactly what business my lover was in. I know he owned a lot of property in various places. He might have been growing drugs on all that land of his for all I knew. But even if he was involved in that business, he was far removed from the street dealer's world and wasn't into drugs himself.

I stayed with Sergio for about six months. Our relationship ended when I wanted a commitment from him and it was clear that he just wanted to have fun with me. I now realize that he must have had other women in his life then, possibly even a wife. But at eighteen I was naive and much less cynical about men than I am now.

When we broke up, Sergio promised to support me for an additional six months. I had no idea then how I was going to make a living in Los Angeles. I only knew that I wanted to stay and figure it out. Sergio paid for an apartment, leased me a car, and gave me some cash. I felt a strong desire to be self-sufficient and make it on my own. When Sergio's support dried up, however, I still didn't know how to do that. I had no education and no skills. It wasn't long, however, before I found out about the many opportunities for a beautiful young woman to sell her body in Hollywood.

LOS ANGELES, 1983

My First Job—In a Massage Parlor

I met a woman who was making a lot of money working in a massage parlor and she suggested I try it. It was a seedy place with red carpets, thin walls, and little rooms. You could hear what was happening in the next room over from yours. Most of the other women who worked there were full-time hookers who walked around in sexy little outfits with G-strings. They were ordinary enough—one woman was even a single mom with a two-year-old to support. At the time I was still pretty innocent. I felt like I was different from the others and didn't belong there. Still, I was determined to give it a try. I needed the money.

The clientele were regular working-class-type guys—truckers with kids and wives. They weren't bad people. My job was to give a guy a massage while naked, do a sexy little dance, and then, if he asked for it, give him either a hand job or a blow job. At first, if a patron didn't ask me for those sexual services, I didn't say a word. I hadn't yet realized I was supposed to entice the guys in order to make more money.

I usually made about $300 a night. A blow job was around $60 or $70 back then and a hand job was $50. On top of this I received the minimum wage for the hours I worked. I made more in one night than I would earn in a week at the kind of job I could get without any skills. It seemed like a lot of money at the time, and I got hooked on making money quickly and easily.

I wanted to be independent, and this kind of money gave me that independence. I didn't want to have to answer to anyone. I didn't have to ask my parents for help, nor did I have to depend on a guy like Sergio again—one who would take care of me financially but who wouldn't make an emotional commitment to me.

I didn't mind the massage parlor work, but what did frighten me was that it was illegal. I heard about a few of these places being raided by the police, and decided to quit before it happened where I worked.

BEVERLY HILLS, 1983

Madam Alex

*S*oon after the massage parlor gig, I met a woman who lived in Beverly Hills, had a nice apartment, and seemed to be doing fairly well. She told me that she worked for the Beverly Hills Madam, Madam Alex—Heidi Fleiss's mentor—and would be happy to introduce me to her. I was nineteen.

Going from the massage parlor to a madam seemed like a natural transition to me. I knew that I didn't have a problem being sexual with strangers and Alex would provide me with a much better-paying class of men. And in Alex's eyes, as well as the eyes and groins of her clients, I was the perfect age.

An older Filipino woman with diabetes, Alex ran her business from her bed. I never saw her in anything but her nightgown, wheeling and dealing women's bodies on her phone. Alex was tough but in some ways she was a very motherly type of madam. If a woman over thirty came to Alex for work, she would tell her in a brutally honest fashion, "You're too old, I can't use you." But Alex also tried to help, like an old-fashioned matchmaker. If she liked the woman, she'd try to fix her up with the right guy. I'd often hear her say, "I might know of a man looking for a mistress." Or better, "I have a guy who is good potential husband material." In addition to her call-girl business, Alex used to set up a lot of women with men who wanted a relationship. She probably did this for the men more than for the women. The men, after all, were her clients and many were old friends. She was very loyal when it came to people she liked.

I know that many aspiring Hollywood actresses worked

for Alex as they tried to make it in their careers. There's been gossip about a few who went on to become famous.

Alex was a coke addict, but somehow she still managed to keep a tight rein on her business. Her cut was 40 percent and she kept careful track of her accounts. My price range when I worked for Alex ranged from $300 up to a high of $3,500. The highest fees usually were for two women having sex for a voyeur.

For a while I was one of Alex's top girls. I saw about six clients a week. She would send me on trips to Monte Carlo, Europe, and the Middle East. I'd come home with expensive luggage, clothes, and jewelry. I told my middle-class parents back in Santa Cruz that I was dating a very wealthy man and had decided not to go to UCLA.

MONTE CARLO, 1983

Arab Men and California Women

Alex, like many Los Angeles madams, had a lot of wealthy Arab clients, men who had so much oil money that they didn't know what to do with it all. The Arab men I met were raised with a kind of respect for women, but that respect is not based on equality or honest treatment. In fact, they seemed to me to really dislike women. They are taught from birth, however, to behave in a certain respectful manner toward them.

One of Alex's clients, an Arab royal of some sort, took me and another girl to Monte Carlo for a week. He was there with his wife, family, and entourage in another hotel and we only saw him for a couple of hours in the evenings. He paid us each $2,000 a day, plus a generous expense account that allowed the two of us to spend an additional total of $6,000 a day on luxury shopping.

After Monte Carlo I also saw the same client in St. Tropez and Cannes. On another trip I stayed on his yacht. As a nineteen-year-old, I thought this life was the best of the best. He was one of my first clients for Alex, and the easy money was really addictive. I was hooked—excuse the pun—and felt very powerful because I could command such high fees.

Another Arab client I saw through Alex would never come inside of me. And he wanted to have anal sex, but that's something I won't do. We compromised on him coming on my back. I enjoyed thinking about how much this man was spending just to come on my back.

There were other Arab clients I saw, however, who made me feel like a low-life hooker. To some, if you're not exactly their cup of tea, they send you packing. One guy was particularly unhappy to see that I was a blonde. Though many Arabs like tall blond California girls, they also think they are dirty. I gave one guy a blow job and he spent the next hour in the bathroom cleansing himself of my infectious filth.

MALIBU, 1984

An Energetic Three-Way with Charlie Minor

Another client Madam Alex sent me to soon after I started working for her was a well-known music business executive, Charlie Minor. He was charming, sweet, and romantic. I met him the first time at Le Dôme, on Sunset, for dinner. He had another girl with him and wanted us to do a threesome after dinner. Naturally we accommodated him for a fee.

About a year later a girlfriend of mine, Tawny, described this guy she was dating without mentioning his name. From the description I knew he was Charlie. I finally said, "It's Charlie Minor, isn't it?"

Tawny wanted to know how I knew and I told her. "You better watch out," I warned her. "He might say all the right things, but he's not looking for a relationship. There's no way. He's not capable of that." She was crushed and a little heartbroken. But I wanted Tawny to know that Charlie Minor was just another player. Despite my sisterly advice, however, she kept seeing him for a while.

One night she invited me to join Charlie and her for dinner at Spago. He didn't remember me from the earlier gig—with as many different women as he had every week, it's no wonder. Afterward we headed to his place in Malibu. Tawny told him that I was a professional and we would have to charge him $500 each for the two of us. He agreed.

Tawny was not a working girl, but she had her own sexual proclivities. She was into domination—she really, really liked to be in control. Charlie apparently was also into the S&M trip. Tawny started the evening by tying him up and pulling out her "toolbox" full of whips with tassels, handcuffs, vibrators, two-ended dildos—the works. My role was to watch and Charlie loved that. For me it was actually a very easy evening. Tawny did it all, finding a use for every one of her sex toys. She was a real trip to watch.

Tawny went out with Charlie a few more times until she realized that I was right about him. There was no future there. Tawny is married now and keeps her husband very busy in the bedroom. Charlie, unfortunately, was murdered by a woman who was in love with him and found him with another woman. Apparently no one had warned her that

Charlie was a player, not the romantic lover he might have seemed to be.

WEST HOLLYWOOD AND
BEVERLY HILLS, 1984

A Glove for Godunov

Another client of Alex's was the late ballet dancer and actor Alexander Godunov. I was running behind schedule the first night I met him. When I arrived at his West Hollywood apartment, he glared at me, obviously upset that I was late and apparently pretty high on drugs. He invited me in. I was immediately horrified by the condition of his apartment. The place was gross—a total pigpen. There were old cartons of food lying around. The furniture and the curtains were filthy. The apartment hadn't been aired out in ages and it smelled awful. I was shocked. Madam Alex had never sent me to a place that was so disgusting.

I wanted to hurry up and get the call over with so I could get out of there. I started to take my clothes off. He kept glaring at me. It was unnerving. I thought that I must not have been his type and asked him if he wanted me to leave. "No, not at all," he assured me. "I just don't want you to undress right now."

He wanted us to get to know each other first. He offered me a drink, and I sat down on the dirty sofa next to him, listening to him talk about himself. He rambled on for a while. Eventually we went into the bedroom.

Alexander asked me to undress and lie on the bed. As I did, he sat in a chair next to the bed and began to mastur-

18

bate. He was still kind of glaring at me while he got himself off, but he didn't touch me. After he came he told me to get dressed and I left. That was the end of our first date. I thought I'd never see him again. Sometimes I'd feel like a call didn't go over too well, and this was certainly one of those times.

My feeling was wrong, however. Alexander Godunov called Alex to ask for me again. The second time I saw him he invited me up to his then-girlfriend Jackie Bisset's house. She was out of town working on a movie. This time he was a very different man, perhaps because he wasn't high.

Jackie's house was extremely beautiful and immaculate—a real change from Alexander's disgusting apartment. A full dinner had been prepared and was waiting in the dining room when I arrived. The champagne flowed as we talked, laughed, and ate. It was originally supposed to be a two-hour job, but Madam Alex had asked me if I would stay the entire night. After I arrived I agreed.

Following the lovely dinner, Alexander ran a bath for me and catered to my every desire. This date was already very different from our first encounter. After the nice evening we'd had so far, he certainly wasn't going to be satisfied with masturbation.

I didn't mind. This was, after all, how I commanded my high fees. The only problem was that he didn't want to use a condom. I was amazed when he said he wouldn't use one. I had no idea where and with whom he'd been. And he definitely didn't know where I had been. I had been around plenty, of course, but always with a condom. He seemed astonished that I refused to let him enter me without protection. He promised me, ''I won't come inside you.'' I was firm, however. ''No way. I don't want even a drop of anything inside me.'' He seemed irritated but finally put on the condom and we had sex. It was rather uneventful—ordinary, everyday fucking. I stayed the night and then left in the morning.

I never saw Godunov after that second date. He said that he would call, but he didn't. I was stunned and saddened by his death a decade later.

LOS ANGELES, 1985

"I Do"

After I'd worked as a call girl for Alex for a while, a friend introduced me to a man who would end up changing my life—my husband. At this point I knew I needed some reality in my life. The world of high-class hooking is so unreal in many ways—the large amounts of money, the different men, the five-star hotels, the blow jobs, the threesomes, the never-ending sexual encounters. I needed stability and grounding and that's what I found with him.

We hit it off immediately. He is very sweet, kind, and just a really good man. Sex isn't the biggest or the best part of our relationship. My husband is fairly conservative sexually and that's fine with me. After fucking people for a living, the sexual aspect was not the most important thing I looked for in a relationship.

My husband is a very handsome man, but that wasn't all that attracted me to him. He has a strong work ethic that I admire. He's focused and confident and has a good sense of who he is. He is also very loving and giving in our relationship.

We had a beautiful wedding in a hotel by the beach. My

friends and family were all there. And the words we said in the ceremony, the vows, were all very meaningful to me. I vowed to love him and to cherish him forever and I still do.

There were sacrifices I had to make in deciding to marry. I had to give up some of the luxuries I had been used to as a highly paid call girl. My husband, who had his own import-export business, makes a good living but he is definitely middle class, unlike the millionaires I was used to. Letting go of that lifestyle was good for me, though. It was part of coming back down to earth again.

I explained to my husband that my line of work had been interior design and that, when I met him, I was between jobs. I also told him that the Louis Vuitton luggage I owned and some of the jewelry I had been given by clients were fake imitations—and he believed me. One time, however, I thought I lost a Rolex watch that had been given to me by a client, and I was really upset. My husband couldn't understand why I was so upset if the watch wasn't the real thing. But he has never checked on the value of anything— he's just not the kind of guy who cares about things like that—and he has never found out about my past with Madam Alex.

After we married he was happy to support me and, at first, that was fine with me. I love to garden and to do oil paintings—I'm not a bad artist. I also love animals and volunteer at an animal shelter. Our married life is pretty routine and normal. We usually go to bed by 9:30 or 10:00 each night. A couple of times a week, we go to the movies together or with friends. I play the company wife when we entertain my husband's work colleagues, but my husband is the better cook and he often cooks if we don't go out for dinner. We usually take a couple of trips together each year. Last year I loved hiking down a volcano in Hawaii.

The only real problem with our life was that my husband travels a lot in his business and I had a lot of time on my hands. I was lonely and perhaps a little bored. I also missed the financial freedom I had always enjoyed. As much as I loved my husband, I didn't like the feeling of being dependent, as I had been with Sergio.

One night, after we had been married about a year, my husband and I were out to dinner. As I looked over at the other diners, I noticed a former client of mine sitting at a table with his wife. When, sometime during the meal, I got up and went to the restroom, my ex-client left his seat at the same time. In the hallway outside of the restroom, he told me that he had been trying to find me. Then he wrote his phone number on the inside of a matchbook cover and gave it to me.

I kept the matchbook for a few months. From time to time I would think about calling him, but I didn't. One day, when my husband was going out of town for a week, I finally decided to call this ex-client. I don't know exactly what made me do it. I had been out of the business for over a year. I think I planned to just talk to him and tell him that I was married and my life had changed.

When he answered the phone he was really sweet and very happy to hear from me. As we talked I remembered that this client was not a bad lover. Maybe I am just easily persuaded when it comes to sex and to earning what I consider to be easy money. I don't know. All I do know is that I agreed to see him, and after that I gradually started working again. If I had never met this man in the restaurant that night, perhaps now my life would be different.

I began to see clients while my husband was out of town or during the day when he was at work. Sometimes when on an overnight job I would tell my husband I was visiting my family in Palm Springs. I didn't go through a madam, but I never had any problem finding clients. There is sort of a working-girl network in L.A. We call each other when we hear about a client who might want more than one woman, when someone has a job she can't do herself, or when a woman knows a guy who wants to meet someone new. Also, there are regular clients who keep in touch with me. I never got back into the business as heavily as I had been in it when I worked for Alex. Now I work only when I feel like it.

I've saved my money in case anything happens to my husband or to our marriage. I have used some of it, however, for little things we need now. My husband gives me a household allowance and thinks I'm great because I manage so well on it. Little does he know where I get the extra money I need.

This may seem hard to believe, but when I'm working I don't feel as though I'm being unfaithful to my husband. Sex with clients, even when I enjoy it, is still work to me. I'm not emotionally involved with my clients and I take care never to let that happen. Of course, most of the men I see aren't interested in emotional involvement. They just want to get off, in a variety of ways with a variety of women.

WEST HOLLYWOOD, 1987

A Quickie with Baryshnikov

Shortly after I started working again, I met the great Russian dancer Mikhail Baryshnikov through a girl-friend who worked for Madam Alex. He wanted two call girls to meet him in his room at the Four Seasons Hotel.

He was one of the sweetest clients I ever had. He seemed

kind of shy and embarrassed about the whole situation. He didn't want to actually have sex with either of us—I think he was afraid of catching something. What he did want was to watch us as we made love to each other. As we went down on each other and pretended to reach orgasm, he watched and then jerked himself off, coming between my breasts.

It was nice and simple. There was not the weird, kinky stuff or toilet sex that a lot of famous guys are into. The whole thing was over in about forty-five minutes. He apologized for rushing off but said he had a dinner date. As we were leaving and he was paying us, he thanked us profusely and told us we were both very beautiful. So was he.

LOS ANGELES, 1988

Charlie Sheen: The Professional John

Charlie Sheen, who was forced to testify at one of Heidi Fleiss's trials, is a well-known john among L.A.'s working girls. Even in the public eye he's probably as famous for his propensity for prostitutes as he is for his films. I was with Charlie only once, years before Heidi was arrested.

Once again the job was with another girl, someone I had met through friends in local call-girl circles. Charlie was dating this woman, although he knew she was a hooker. One night she asked me to join them and we all met at a hotel.

Charlie was kinky, but not in a sick way. He simply likes role playing and different kinds of sex. I had been told not to wear any makeup or stockings. "Just wear some knee-socks. Look preppy," my friend suggested. Charlie particularly liked to direct the show. First he dressed us both and did our makeup. Then he told me to watch while he had sex with my friend.

My girlfriend was totally in love with Charlie. He later dumped her and married model Donna Peele, who then quickly divorced him. My friend was heartbroken when Charlie left her. Even though she was a hooker, she had fallen for Charlie Sheen in the worst way. For her, sex with Charlie was for love, not for money. For me, of course, it was for money.

I was paid $1,000 for my participation that night. Charlie was always very good financially to his girls. He has leased cars and purchased gold watches and other jewelry for them. But he's always had lots of women and he has hurt more than a few of them. He would easily convince a woman, as he did my girlfriend, that she was really "the one." Even a working girl, however, can get hurt by a guy's empty promises. Charlie will probably remarry, but I'm sure he'll never be monogamous. Like the other Charlie I knew, Charlie Minor, Charlie Sheen is a player.

BEVERLY HILLS, 1989

A Gift for Don Johnson

I was a present for Don Johnson, given to him by one of his friends. The catch for me was that Don wasn't supposed to know I was a hooker. Once again the job was a two-girl thing, which, if my own experience is any indication, is really the rage with Hollywood actors.

We met at Don's bungalow in the Beverly Hills Hotel. At first he seemed a little nervous but still was very charming and considerate. He knew the other girl and that helped make things easier. She was very beautiful and definitely a professional, but one who didn't come across too whor-ish or businesslike.

Don Johnson was the opposite of Charlie Sheen. He just wanted us to be natural. Unlike most actors I have met, he wasn't into acting and directing in the bedroom. He simply wanted to watch two women enjoy each other, and we proceeded to do just that. As we alternately went down on each other, Don sat there mesmerized. He was getting very turned on by what he was viewing.

After this beautiful woman and I had been having sex together for a while, I went into the bathroom. When I came out, the scenario had changed. Don was screwing the other girl and he wanted me to watch. While he fucked her, he kept telling each of us how beautiful, wonderful, and exceptional we were. He seemed to really get off on it all. "This is the best experience," he burst out at one point.

I watched them have sex for the next hour and a half. All the while he kept flattering us both with superlatives. After two hours I left, and have never seen him since. Eventually I was paid by Don's friend who had furnished me for the little get-together. I don't know if Don ever knew I was a gift.

LOS ANGELES, 1990

Doing It with Don Henley

*A*t a party following a Bryan Adams concert, a girl-friend introduced me to Don Henley. At first he seemed like a very interesting man. He talked about environmental issues and about saving the rainforests and endangered animals, and I felt like I had a lot in common with him. But the minute he started partying, he completely changed. His intellect vanished and he was suddenly all dick. Bryan Adams wasn't into the drug and sex scene that Don was into, so he left the party before midnight. Henley was then all alone with a group of working girls and he loved it.

Don, my girlfriend, and the other three women were doing a lot of coke and Quaaludes, but I wasn't. I've never been into the drug scene. I don't like the feeling of being out of control, especially when I'm working.

Henley offered me $1,000 for my services, which was not that much considering how insatiable he was. He simply couldn't get enough. There were five of us servicing him at the same time. One girl sucked his dick and another was sucking his toes while he was eating yet another one. He wanted all of us to be really involved and act like we were into it, which was ridiculous. In fact, it was just one big sex circus and we were performers, not because we loved it but because we were being paid.

Four of the girls as well as Don were totally coked out of their minds and the drugs made it an all-night thing. For me it was really draining because I didn't have uppers to keep me going like the rest of them.

Don finally climaxed after about two hours of every kind of sex act imaginable. Then he fell asleep. I wanted to go home, but my girlfriend said to stick around and get some sleep, because when he woke up he would want to do it all over again. I figured I'd better stay since I was hired for the night. Sure enough, when he awakened, we were soon back at it again. One woman was giving him a blow job, his fingers were up another woman, two women were playing with each other. It was the circus again—Act Two.

I really earned every cent of my fee that night.

Unfortunately, in the morning he was out cold, so I had to leave without my money.

About a week later my girlfriend called me and said to meet her at Don's house to pick up my check. I knew what that meant. There would be more circus acts before the check delivery. I didn't mind getting and giving a little more, but this time I was determined to set a time limit.

When I got to the house, Don offered me a glass of wine and told me how terrific I had been the other night. Right away I said, "I have two hours. If you want to get together, we can do whatever you want, but that is my limit." My friend and I ended up having a little threesome with Don. She and I were together and then he fucked her. After about an hour and a half it was over. He paid me $1,000 for each night and I left. That was the last time I saw Don Henley. He told my girlfriend that he didn't care for my time constraints. It put too much pressure on him. I was definitely not the type for his all-night parties.

I have many girlfriends who know Don and some who still see him. He's a decent guy in many ways. He has helped out a few girls I know who were going through tough times. But, like so many men in this town, he won't admit to the sexual stuff he is into. He called *You'll Never Make Love in This Town Again* trash, but from my experience the stories in that book, as well as this one, reflect exactly what it's like to be with good old Don. He should just look in the mirror and admit the truth.

LOS ANGELES, 1991

Bob Broadcast's Noontime Blow Jobs

Another guy in the entertainment industry who likes to have sex with more than one woman is someone I'll call "Bob Broadcast." He told me he does film reviews on CNN.

I saw him several times and it was always the same. Bob would come over to my girlfriend's apartment in a big rush. He was always on a deadline and only had an hour to spare. He would rush in and say, "I want it all, in one hour or less." Then he would start to undress and reveal the red ladies' panties that he always wore. Next he wanted the two of us to show him our lingerie. We stripped to our sexy bras and panties and then pretended that we were really into each other. We would rub our bodies against one another and use our fingers on each other. He always went nuts at that point, sniffing our undergarments with his big nose as we faked our orgasms.

Another thing Bob liked was to be spanked with wooden paddles. When it was time for him to come over, we always had our Ping-Pong paddles ready. It was a great way for me to unleash my anger. He wanted us to beat him as hard as we could, and we did.

Neither of us ever fucked him, but we each would give him a blow job. Taking turns, one of us would suck his dick and the other would tempt him with lingerie. With his red panties down around his ankles, he would play with our bras and panties as he came. It was quite a sight.

That was Bob Broadcast's big erotic noontime break. When it was over, we got dressed and stifled our laughter as we watched him pull up his panties, put on his business suit and tie, and rush back to the station to meet his deadline.

VENICE, 1991

Robert Duvall's Oscar-Winning Performance

About five years ago I started seeing Academy Award–winning actor Robert Duvall. Although Robert pays me whenever we meet, I don't believe that he thinks of our dates as prostitution. To him it seems more like he's giving me a gift at the end of the evening. That gift just happens to be a $500 check.

In this business you have to be open to all kinds of different scenarios. The first time we were together, it didn't take a rocket scientist to realize that Robert got off on talking dirty. I went right to it, telling him that I was his "little motherfucker." He loved that line and yelled back at me, "Fuck me you motherfucking bitch! Suck this big hard cock, and suck it now!"

Sex with Robert is always theatrical. He's very dramatic, as though he's playing a role. When his clothes are off, he almost seems like a different person from who he is when he's dressed. He becomes an animal—a very sexy, wild beast on a woman hunt. Then he gets dressed and once again he's mild and friendly. It's as though I've done an exorcism on him.

Robert has always treated me well. When he comes back into town and we get together, he is very sweet, telling me how much he has missed me. And in bed, at the moment of climax, he insists on knowing if I care for him. Of course I know I'm not the only woman in his life. He was married and going through a divorce when we first met. He also likes one of my friends and I know he's crazy about black women—not light-skinned ones, but women whose skin is really dark.

Robert is a great actor. He's very natural and gives an

honest performance on–screen and off. Sometimes I see ex-pressions on his face in his films that are exactly how he looks when he's about to come. Recently my husband and I rented *The Godfather*. As we watched the movie I smiled to myself, thinking of him running around the hotel room naked, talking dirty. I don't know which performance was better.

BEL AIR, 1992

The Devil: Don Simpson

*S*ex, drugs, and blockbuster movies put Don Simpson, the late super-producer, in the spotlight during his Hol-lywood reign. Simpson loved to be the focus, the main man. In his own demonic, overblown egotistical way, he usually commanded an audience in this screwed–up town. I didn't find him the least bit interesting, however. To me, he was a very sick man and just another john.

I first met him when a friend invited me to join a group of working girls who were going to Simpson's house. When I arrived, there were perhaps a dozen women and Simpson. He was talking to one girl who obviously wanted to be an actress. She was telling him that she would do any-thing to reach her dream. I'm sure he was thinking of all the things he would soon get her to do in hopes of getting his help.

I recognized a few women in the group, many of whom, I'm sure, knew his M.O. A couple of the women there looked like street-hooker types. Since it was my first time in this scene, I was paying close attention to the girls who seemed to know the drill. I was also a bit irritated because I didn't really feel like hanging out and partying with these people. I just wanted to do my thing, get paid, and get out.

Finally we all got naked. Then the drugs came out and an evil look shone from Simpson's eyes. He was the master drug lord of the moment. Though I don't usually like to use the term, most of his naked prey were definitely "coke whores." It was sad how they were hooked the moment the cocaine appeared. It was Simpson's way of keeping these girls there and making them do whatever he wanted.

I told Simpson that I didn't do drugs and he gave me a nasty look, like I was holier-than-thou. I'm not. I'm simply not a drug user. Simpson resented the advantage that being sober gave me—he couldn't control me with his coke, only with his money.

He kept hounding me about the coke. "Are you sure you don't want to try some? It won't hurt you. You'll feel good." I continued to decline his offer. It's very bizarre to be around heavy coke users. It feels as though they are spinning out of control all around you.

The party continued. Naked women were everywhere, doing everything the master wanted. At one point I walked into a room and found Simpson on top of a bed with a girl standing over him, peeing on him. She urinated all over his body and his face, soaking the sheets beneath him.

He saw me and said, "Come over here and lick the pee off my face and body." I was completely grossed out. "No thank you," I mumbled. "I don't think I can do that." He got angry, jumping up and yelling at me, "I'm paying you to come here and do this. Don't think you're going to get out of it." The whole thing almost made me vomit. I wanted to say, "Get over yourself, you're disgusting." Instead I tried to be very professional. I started to get dressed and said, "I just can't do that." I was ready to leave and not get paid. I told him I didn't need the money that bad.

Suddenly his tune changed. He tried to be nice. He asked me to stay. I told him that if he took a shower and washed the urine off of himself, I'd have sex with him. It ruffled his feathers that I was so demanding. He didn't like a whore making demands on him. For some reason, however, he did what I asked.

After Simpson showered, he got in bed with a couple of the other girls. I joined them and gave him a blow job. I must have sucked that hard-core Hollywood dick for an hour, but he never came. It was all the drugs, I suppose, that kept him from coming. No matter how long I sucked this man—himself one of the biggest cocksuckers in town—nothing happened. It was now about three or four in the morning and I had been there since ten. Even though I was being paid $1,500 for my time, I told him I wanted to go. He was irritated and wanted me to stay longer. "You're not on a fucking time clock," he growled. Finally he paid me and I left. You can be sure that I took a long shower when I got home.

BEL AIR, 1992

Don Simpson: Take Two

Don kept asking me to come back. I think I was a challenge to him. I wouldn't lick pee off him. I wouldn't do drugs. I was a little harder to control than many of the other girls, and he must have found that exciting.

Finally I agreed. I figured that he liked to watch two women together a lot and that was something I didn't mind doing. I thought I could handle going to his house one more time. After all, the money was so good. It would take me three, four, or even five jobs to earn what he paid for one night.

The night I returned to his house I found Simpson and another girl already there. She was one of his regulars, an experienced dominatrix. I think her name was Dakota. She had very pale skin, black hair, and was extremely masculine-looking.

As I walked through the house I discovered other women in various rooms. I saw one girl getting fucked with a cucumber by another one, the latter probably a dominatrix in training. I saw people in handcuffs, wearing leather, and carrying whips and stuff like that. Most of the night I just watched what was going on.

Finally I had to earn my $1,500. Simpson told me to lie naked on a bed, facedown. He wanted to tie me up. I told him that I really don't like to be tied up or blindfolded or anything like that. I get claustrophobic. He promised that the ties would be very loose and I would be able to get out whenever I wanted.

That's not what happened. He secured me very tightly to the bed so I couldn't move. The more I struggled to get loose, the more excited Simpson seemed to get. The dominatrix whipped me and slapped me until at some point she and Simpson turned me over. Dakota then started rubbing her body on mine, genital to genital. She did everything. She used a vibrator and later she strapped on a two-ended dildo and fucked me with it.

Simpson was watching and getting more and more turned on by all of this. Then he got on the bed on top of us, holding his penis in his hands. I thought that he was going to come or urinate. Sure enough, he peed all over us. I was grateful he missed my face, but the rest of me was covered with his urine.

As he pissed he held his cock, rocking back and forth

simulating a fucking motion. Then he jacked himself off and came all over us, right on top of his own urine. I felt like a toilet.

After he came he let me up. I showered and got dressed as quickly as I could. Simpson was very cordial as I was leaving. He paid me my $1,500 and said in a normal, polite tone of voice, "See ya later." It was creepy. It made me wonder how many average-looking guys, who seemed nice enough, were really sickos like this man.

I hurried out of there and never went back. He had gotten his humiliating, degrading way with me. I went back that second time because I thought I could handle it. I believed I could separate myself from what went on at that house, that I could just leave a situation like that and not feel any aftereffects. Now I know there are always some residual effects from this kind of experience. I was strong enough in who I am not to be deeply traumatized, as were so many girls who spent time around Simpson. But from that point on I decided not to put myself in that kind of situation ever again. I knew other women who had gotten quite messed up around him. I didn't want to push it.

Overdosing was an easy way out for a man as warped as Don Simpson. I'm glad, though, that he's no longer up in his big house in Bel Air torturing women. His Hollywood colleagues all praised him when he died, but I loathed the man.

BEVERLY HILLS AND PALM SPRINGS, 1990S

Alan Smithee's Scatological Obsessions

I first met Alan Smithee, an infamous Hollywood producer, at a party held in his house during a Mike Tyson fight. A girlfriend in the business had invited me, so I expected something business-wise to happen during the evening.

When we arrived at Smithee's gorgeous Beverly Hills house, there were lots of celebrities—everyone from Jack Nicholson to attorney Robert Shapiro, who had once represented Smithee. My friend and I found Alan in his bedroom with about five other working girls. A few male agents also were there, and he seemed to be trying to fix up the agents and the call girls. When we entered the room, Smithee seemed very charming . . . until he asked me to lift up my blouse and expose my breasts. I suppose he was trying to impress the other guys and show them what he could make the women do. I wouldn't do it. I told him I would take off my shirt in private but not in front of all these people.

At one point Robert Shapiro came into the bedroom to thank Smithee, the host, and tell him that he was leaving. Shapiro seemed like a real gentleman who wasn't at all into Alan's sex and drug scene.

I left the bedroom and went back out to the main rooms where I ate some food and mingled with people. The party wound down and, at the end of the evening, Alan asked me to join him and another woman for a *ménage*. He was too coked out himself to do anything but watch. He couldn't get an erection. I earned about $500 or $600 and left that night thinking he wasn't a bad client. I would soon learn, however, about the real Alan Smithee.

The next time I went to his house, he was also very charming. He showed me around the place and brought out numerous magazine articles about himself and his films. The quintessential Hollywood producer, he was filled with stories about himself and his work.

He wanted to give me pills he called "water pills," which he told me would help me lose extra water-weight. In truth, what he was really hoping the pills would do was cause me to urinate frequently. He also wanted me to eat a lot of dates and other fruit. I don't have to tell you what that was supposed to cause me to do.

That night I learned how sick Alan is. He wanted me to pee and shit on him. I told him I wasn't into that stuff, but he kept pressuring me. Finally I agreed to try peeing on his foot in the shower. I don't understand why anything like that would give anyone pleasure, but since he was paying me $1,500 for the night, I tried to accommodate him. We stepped into the shower and I started to urinate. Not content to just stand there, he kneeled under me and opened his mouth. He swallowed some of my urine, and the rest ended up in his hair. Next thing I knew, Alan got right out of the shower without even washing his hair. I stayed the whole night and never saw him wash himself off. He went to a meeting the next morning with urine in his hair.

The third time I saw Alan, he had invited me, along with several other working girls, to Palm Springs. He was in the middle of working on a book about his life, and he wanted to impress his co-author with how many women were in love with him. Alan had the whole thing scripted out. He said to me, "Tell him [the writer] that you're in love with me and that you can't stop thinking about me." I am not exactly the best actress, and I can't play quite that dumb. When I met the writer I just said that Alan was a great guy and I cared about him.

Cocaine use was rampant that weekend, as it always was with Alan. He did so much cocaine that when he went into the bathroom to brush his teeth, he'd come out with toothpaste and foam all over his face. He was almost numb from the drugs and didn't know what he was doing half the time. Two of the women, who were staying in another bungalow from where he and I and a redheaded woman were, got so high during the weekend that they went berserk. They got in a fight, threw chairs through the windows, and completely trashed the place.

Meanwhile, in our bungalow the redhead was really into Alan's toilet sex. She not only peed on him, she shit on him. He just loved it. He put his fingers up her rear end as she was having the bowel movement. Then he actually ate her shit. The scene was way too gross for me. Once again, he never even showered or cleaned his fingernails afterward. It was not a pretty picture. I can't think of him today without thinking about his dirty fingernails and his urine-soaked hair.

Alan seemed to like me because I was healthier than most of the women he had around him. At the time I knew him, his friends Jack Nicholson and Warren Beatty were having babies and he decided he wanted to have one, too. He said to me during one of our encounters, "I'd like you to have one of my babies." I joked back, "Oh yeah? Would you visit it?"

After the Palm Springs weekend he kept calling me. He wanted to support me and get me an apartment. Of course, I hadn't told him my real situation. He kept telling me that I could be a really successful actress with his help. I never returned his calls and, after a while, he quit calling.

Alan is just a very pathetic man who happens to have a lot of power in an industry run by many pathetic, sick men.

BEVERLY HILLS, THE 1990S

Quickies with Other Professionals

*M*ost of the men I see are not like Alan Smithee. Lawyers, doctors, and other professionals, many of them local big shots, comprise a large percentage of my clients. They've been married twenty years, own a house in Beverly Hills, and have two kids in school. I see them on lunch breaks, on weekends after golf, or whenever they can fit me into their busy schedules. I rarely have intercourse with these men—I just give their dicks a good workout with my hand or my mouth. Many, however, don't even want oral sex. Perhaps they think that it is too dangerous or too intimate. A hand job, however, is quick and easy. It's over in half an hour, the client is satisfied, and I'm $300 richer. Another thing these men like about this arrangement is that if their wives ever accuse them of cheating, they can honestly say they haven't "fucked" anyone. Beverly Hills wives should be a little more specific in their accusations if they really want to know what their husbands are up to.

One of my longtime clients is very funny. He's a medical doctor and he is extremely afraid of sexually transmitted diseases, especially AIDS. I appreciate his concern because I, too, am very careful. But this man is so cautious that he wears rubber gloves when he touches me. He also tells me that his name is Bill, even though I know his name is Mark. Maybe he has convinced himself that he doesn't have to feel guilty about seeing a call girl if he uses another name. I don't know. I do know he's married.

Bill likes a good blow job. He lies on the bed with a condom on his penis and rubber gloves on his hands. I can't begin to tell you how clinical it all is. There is never any kissing, of course. And I have to be very careful. If I get a drop of saliva on his pores, he freaks out. I can't blame him, though. Even if he can't be faithful to his wife, at least he's protecting himself and her from diseases—even the common cold.

LOS ANGELES, 1993

Betrayal before the C-Section

*D*oing what I do makes it hard for me to believe that any man is completely faithful to his wife. Perhaps some men remain faithful, but I can't imagine that it's more than a very small percentage of them. I've run into clients who are with their wives and kids in the grocery store. To everyone else, they look like the perfect little family, but I know that, the day before, I sucked the husband's dick.

The most despicable thing I've seen one of these men do to his wife was something that happened a few years ago. A professional whom I had been seeing for a while called me up one day. He told me that he had just dropped off his wife at the hospital. She was going in for a C-section, which was scheduled for 2 P.M. It would take a while for her to get prepped and ready to deliver, so he wanted me to meet him at his house at 11 A.M. I was shocked. If ever I wanted to say no to a client, it was at that moment. But I didn't, rationalizing that he would just call someone else instead. I met him at his house and fucked him in his wife's bed, while she was lying in the hospital waiting to deliver their child.

The worst part of doing what I do, for me, is thinking about the wives. Most of my clients are just average guys who want a little something extra on the side. I see pictures of their wives and kids around my clients' houses or offices, and I know that what I'm doing with these men would hurt their wives if they knew. If a woman found out that her husband was meeting a prostitute every Wednesday after golf, it could shatter their marriage. Of course, I again think to myself that if the husband wasn't calling me, he would just find another hooker to call. And I want to make the money now, before I'm too old. I guess money, for me (as it seems to be for most people in this town), is more important than just about anything else.

The Producer's Wife

*M*en, generally, go to prostitutes. So it is very rare for call girls to have women clients. I have had two in my career.

The first is married and is, in fact, one of the most prominent wives in town. I'll call her Heather. Heather's husband is a mega-rich, mega-successful mega-workaholic in the entertainment business. To the outside world they live a charmed life. They have an incredible house, servants, and the best of everything.

I met Heather through a mutual friend, another client of mine. He must have told her what I do, and somehow she decided to call me.

When I visit her at home, I usually go there with health products—as though I'm a service person of some sort—so the servants and people around the house aren't suspicious. Often we meet somewhere else. I think her motivation for calling me is that she's lonely and looking for some sort of intimacy in her life. Her husband is always working, and I've heard a rumor that he's gay. I don't know if the latter is true, but I do know that they've been married a very long time and she hasn't gotten what she needs from him for years.

Being with a woman client is a much different experience for me than being with a man. For one thing, Heather's emotions seem to run higher than those of my male clients. When she and I are together, she acts as if she's been really boxed up for a long time, and often cries when she reaches orgasm.

Heather is very kind to me. It's interesting that she chose a woman rather than a man to fulfill her sexual needs because I don't think she even considers herself bisexual. I suspect it's because women are more sensitive, and she needs that warm, emotional part as well as the physical part.

BEVERLY HILLS, 1990S

The Other Woman

The only other woman client I have ever had is a very successful lawyer and a closeted lesbian. I met her through mutual friends. She's extremely beautiful and most people would never suspect that she's gay. She and I went out for a drink one night. We were talking and she sort of told me her life story. I felt very comfortable with her so I told her a little about what I do.

She was very intrigued. At one point she asked, "If I give you five hundred dollars would you spend the night with me?" I said yes—and I wouldn't even charge her that much.

To her this arrangement was like a dream come true. But after a while she got too emotionally involved. She was a really neat person and I really cared about her, too. If I wasn't married and if I thought that I could ever be with a woman, I would have chosen her. For both our sakes, however, I had to cut it off. It's important that I don't get attached to clients, and I didn't want to see her get hurt.

HOLLYWOOD, 1994

Mike Mogul: More Hollywood Decadence

There's another Hollywood producer I see who is also very sick. Like his friend, the late Don Simpson, this man is a successful and prolific producer of well-known films, whose credits may include such films as *That's Entertainment, All That Jazz, Altered States* and more recently, *L.A. Story,* and *Universal Soldier.* He's been around Hollywood a long time and served briefly as studio president at both MGM and Columbia. He has a beautiful house in the Hollywood Hills that is filled with exquisite works of art. He's highly educated and enjoys surrounding himself with intelligent people. I'm afraid to use his name, however, because I think he might try to retaliate against me somehow. I'll call him Mike Mogul.

The first time I saw him was when I went up to his house with another girl. He had a five-course dinner waiting for us and together we drank wine, ate, and talked. Then he told us to go into the bedroom and put on robes. He has a vast collection of beautiful silk robes. He also has a box containing every kind of sex toy imaginable.

Mike likes to direct the show, as do so many Hollywood producer and actor types. He gets excited about watching two women together using a two-ended dildo. And he also can get a little rough in the bedroom—for example, he enjoys pinching women's nipples.

Mike is bizarre in another way as well. He hires call girls

all the time, but he doesn't want them to act like call girls. He gets angry if a woman takes off her clothes too soon or, as he puts it, "acts like a whore." In his twisted brain, he wants to believe that the women he hires really care for him.

The most humiliating part of being with Mike is how he parades me past visitors and friends just after we have sex. I would often arrive on a call to find a group of guys over at his house. These guys sat in one room while Mike and I had sex in another room. After we finished he'd tell me to walk past his friends. So I would, and he'd tell them how good I was. It felt so degrading. I really felt bad each time that happened.

Mike has gotten heavily into drugs in recent years. He has also run into some financial trouble, which has inhibited his ability to hire prostitutes. When I first met him, he used to have two women a night for as many as five or six nights every week. He paid us each $1,000 then, so Mike was spending $2,000 a night and $10–12,000 a week. It adds up fast.

Because Mike is short on funds, I've dropped my price for him to $500, and I don't see him nearly as often. I know he also gets women drug addicts to help satisfy his sex addiction, whom he pays with drugs instead of cash. Maybe he'll end up like his friend Don Simpson one day—it seems to be the direction he's headed. It wouldn't be a great loss to society.

WEST HOLLYWOOD, 1995

Kerry Packer's Fringe Benefits

*A*ustralian business magnate Kerry Packer is extremely generous to his male employees. Some of the quickest, easiest money I ever made was working for Kerry, providing blow jobs for young associates of his who were in Tinseltown on business.

One day I got a call from someone who worked for Kerry requesting that I show up at the Four Seasons Hotel on a particular night later that week. I arrived as directed at the room of a young man who was about twenty-three. I gave him the usual blow job. He was very energetic and came twice in the hour. Then he called one of his co-workers staying in the hotel and I rushed off to his room for a blow job.

Kerry Packer called me himself the next day to ask if everything was okay and if I was being treated properly. He was very considerate. The following evening I returned to the Four Seasons to service two more Packer employees. These gentlemen had dinner plans at eight. I arrived at seven and sucked them both off in the hour. My earnings—$1,000 for each night.

Packer was certainly generous to his Down-Under boys, giving them each an expense account with an allowance for hookers. After all, they were in Hollywood—why shouldn't they do what all the guys in Hollywood do?

What Do Men Really Want?

*P*rostitution is like many other businesses—you learn as you earn. As a working girl, I've learned a lot about men, and I feel like I know what they really want, in the bedroom at least.

First of all, I'm now much more aware of the differences between men. Some want intimacy and affection, to be hugged and kissed and to feel like you care about them. Others just want a quick fuck, a hand job, or a blow job and to be on their way.

A lot of men, particularly the married ones, are sexually repressed. They come to me to fulfill their fantasies and be allowed to feel as if they are the greatest studs in the world. With me they act out things in the bedroom that their wives either don't want to do with them, or that they are afraid to ask their wives to do. The poor wife, who sees her husband day in and day out, may not have the patience to tell him things like, "You've got the largest cock in the world, and you're getting my pussy hot." Or, "I wish my girlfriend were here to watch us while you do this" (a line that seems to please a lot of men every time). Unlike my clients' wives, I don't mind indulging my clients' egos and acting out their fantasies with them—I get paid very well to do so.

A lot of married men also seem to need to talk to me about their wives. In the heat of orgasm, as they're pounding me with the organ that is supposed to be reserved for their wife, they'll talk about how they want me to eat her pussy. I'm sure it would not be much consolation to a woman that her husband was thinking about her at that moment. One man I see always talks about wanting me to eat his wife while he's fucking me. He's never arranged this particular situation, but it really excites him to think about it.

Perhaps the biggest turn-on for men—at least if you count the number of guys who ask for it and the price we hookers can command for doing it—is watching two women make love. Men seem to be really intrigued by lesbian lovemaking. Deep down I think they believe that every woman wants to be with another woman.

Personally, I like being with women. I consider myself

bisexual and, in a working situation, I find it much easier to be with another woman. When another woman is present, I'm not alone with the guy and the whole focus isn't on me. The other woman is there to help me out.

Sometimes guys just like to watch, but usually after they watch they like to participate. Sometimes they like both women to fuck them. Other times they like to fuck one woman while the other watches. The men always call the shots, of course, because they are paying. Being in control seems to be a big part of the turn-on for men. They can't always order their wives around, but two prostitutes will accommodate their every whim.

Men also really like blow jobs. So do I, because they are easier, faster, usually safer, and always less intimate. I don't feel, as I do with intercourse, that someone who I may or may not like has invaded my body. It also seems to me like a more honest transaction. I am there to service the man and to be paid. When I just do a blow job, I don't have to fake my own orgasm if I'm not into it.

Obviously some men like the kinkier stuff, and are into sex toys and S&M, but they aren't the average client. Those men are out there and when I find them, I don't always go back.

In my line of work, an orgasm—and whatever it takes to achieve one—is what men really want. They want this so much that they're willing to pay me and other women a lot of money, they're willing to jeopardize their marriages, to risk public humiliation, and many times even risk endangering their lives through disease. That may seem strange to some people, but, of course, I risk the same things for the money.

LOS ANGELES, 1996

Lessons

I got into prostitution for the easy money. With Sergio, my first boyfriend, I developed a taste for luxurious and expensive things. Then I worked in a massage parlor and made more money in one night than most women I knew made in a week. I suppose it's kind of like kids in the ghetto who start dealing drugs. They look around at the options that are open to them, and they realize that they can make more money faster the illegal way.

That's what it was like for me. I wanted money. I wanted to be financially independent. After Sergio, I never wanted to depend on a man to support me. Although my husband technically supports me now, through prostitution I have saved enough money so that if anything ever happens to my marriage, I will be all right financially.

During the period just after I married, before I went back to work as a call girl, I considered pursuing an acting career. That idea didn't last long. Hollywood is too much of a casting couch town. I realized that the women who get ahead are the ones who have fucked the right people. In the movie business, it's not just who you know, it's who you fuck. If I were single and pursuing a career, perhaps I could have done that. It certainly isn't that much different from prostitution. But, as a married woman, I couldn't do the schmoozing and socializing that leads to the fucking that leads to the screen roles. Of course, there are exceptions in Hollywood as there are everywhere, but from what I've seen—and I've seen a lot—that's how women make it. For guys, movie business success might mean starting in the mailroom, but for women, it too often means starting in the bedroom.

I'm grateful for one thing about myself—that I was never interested in drugs. So many women earn fantastic amounts of money as call girls and then, in order to numb themselves to what they are doing, throw it all away on drugs. I want too much to be in control to take drugs. When I'm on a call, I want to know what is going on. If I let myself get high on drugs, I might let some guy fuck me without a condom and end up pregnant, or worse, with AIDS or any number of sexually transmitted diseases. I have always treated prostitution as a business. To succeed at it, I want to be at my best when on the job, certainly not high or spaced out on drugs. In that very practical sense, I have been successful at my business.

The addictions that keep me in this business are the money and the excitement. Living a double life and getting away with it gives me an adrenaline rush. It's the stuff of good spy novels.

Another thing that has probably kept me in the business is that I truly enjoy sex with another woman and that's always a big part of being a call girl. Although I don't consider myself a lesbian, I do believe that once you've been with a woman, it's very hard not to want that. There's something really special about it.

Regardless of what I like about being a hooker, I would not wish this life on my worst enemy. In addition to the obvious physical dangers, prostitution is hazardous to a person's moral health. I'm not sure if it should be a crime as it is now, but it certainly isn't the most positive thing in the world—either for the women or the men.

Though it may sound strange to people who have read my story, I consider myself a feminist. I believe that if we lived in a world where there were true financial equality between men and women, where women had as many opportunities as men to earn good money, then women would rarely make the choice to fuck men for a living. I want to have children one day, and if I have a daughter I don't want her to go to school for years and years only to end up in a dead-end job. I want her to have more of a chance to be independent and financially successful than the women of my generation.

The process of writing this book has made me really think about my life—about the risks I am taking, about the negative consequences of my husband ever finding out what I do, about the opportunities that would arise if and when I no longer spent so much of my time working as a call girl. Right now I'm seeing very few clients, and I hope to stop working altogether one day soon. I don't know what the future will hold for me if I give up what I have done for so long now. I might want to go to college. I definitely hope to have a family. My husband and I have talked about one day opening a bed-and-breakfast in some beautiful place. There are so many ways I believe I can make a contribution to society.

To fulfill any of my dreams for the future, however, I know I must end this chapter in my life once and for all. It won't be easy for me, but I hope I will be ready to stop selling my body very, very soon.

Lisa

HEIGHT:	*5′8″*
HAIR:	*Blond*
EYES:	*Blue*
WEIGHT:	*120*
PROFESSION:	*Call girl*
BORN:	*Beverly Hills, California*
HOBBIES:	*Skiing and dancing*
EDUCATION:	*Accepted to UCLA; never attended*
FIRST SEXUAL EXPERIENCE:	*At fifteen with a skier who was twenty-eight*
GOALS & DESIRES:	*To have a business career*
SEXUAL FANTASY:	*To be with the man I love every night*
DRUGS:	*Cocaine, crack, food*
HAPPIEST MEMORY:	*Getting all my legal problems taken care of and having a clean record again*
WORST EXPERIENCE:	*Being abducted and gang-raped by Crips while out buying drugs*
SEX PARTNERS:	*Sylvester Stallone, Alexander Godunov, Steven Tyler, Berry Gordy, Adnan Khashoggi, and more*

Your Average High-Class Call Girl

As a kid, I definitely did not hope to be a call girl and a drug addict when I grew up. And I don't think most other women in this business had such aspirations, either. As a Jewish girl from the San Fernando Valley's upper-middle-class community of Encino, I assumed I would marry a nice Jewish attorney or doctor, live in the hills, and have two kids. That's not what happened. I'm thirty-five now, and most of my adult life—until a year and a half ago—I have worked as a call girl.

Most call girls have a lot in common. Just as salesgirls in department stores all have bad feet from standing for so many hours, prostitutes tend to be very self-destructive people who need a lot of attention. Some of us are more honest about ourselves and will admit to such shortcomings, but others are still in denial and can't yet talk truthfully about themselves.

Every one of us started out, like other children, looking for love and affection. We didn't get that love and affection from our parents, nor did we get it from our first boyfriends. After a while we learned how to protect ourselves from getting hurt emotionally—by selling ourselves. When I first started hooking, I used to think, "If all this guy wants is to fuck me, if he doesn't love me, then it's all right because he paid me. He can't hurt me because I'm getting something out of it: money."

Most call girls are very attractive women who come from dysfunctional families, often where there were divorces and where one or more forms of abuse—physical, verbal, or emotional—occurred. Or perhaps there was simply neglect by the parents at critical times in a young girl's life. As a result of abuse and family problems, most call girls also end up with addictive personalities and many have eating disorders.

Beyond addictions to drugs and alcohol, prostitution itself also becomes an addiction for call girls. We become addicted to the money, to the attention, to the excitement, to the freedom to do what we want, and to not having to work nine-to-five in a career that will get us nowhere.

Like other call girls I know, prostitution has taken me a lot of places—everywhere from five-star hotels in Europe to the Los Angeles County jail.

ENCINO, CALIFORNIA

A Nice Jewish Girl from Encino

My mother grew up in London during the forties and came to America with her family when she was nine. When she was twenty-three, she moved from New York to Los Angeles, where she immediately met my father, a successful forty-year-old businessman. She became pregnant with me and they married.

Both my parents are Jewish—Reform Jews. The family belonged to a well-known society-type temple, and we fasted for the High Holidays, but other than that we weren't very religious. But being compatible in their attitude about religion didn't mean my parents were compatible in other ways. They separated for the first time when I was ten years old. I knew they were unhappy, but they never talked to my sister and me about it. I never learned from them how men and women were supposed to communicate.

I was a bright child and an active one. I was on the swim team and the diving team; I took gymnastics and ballet, as well as skating and guitar lessons. I had a horse of my own, and for my fourteenth birthday my parents gave me a Saks Fifth Avenue credit card. I was given all the material things I wanted, but the emotional support was not there. I would say, "Mom, I love you," and she'd just say, "Thank you." She didn't tell me she loved me, too.

When I was a teenager, my mom took out a great deal

of her unhappiness on me. She was verbally abusive, saying things to me like, "You're always going to be a loser. You're never going to get married and if you do, you'll end up divorced." She also used to complain, "I wish I never had you." Or, "It's your fault that I'm in this marriage." Besides this frequent verbal abuse, she would knock me around, pull my hair, and scratch my face. One time she hit me and I ran into the kitchen, pulled a knife out of the drawer, and screamed at her, "Get away from me right now!" Life with my mother was hell from the time I was thirteen until I moved out of her house at the age of nineteen.

Sometimes my younger sister, who is a more easygoing person, tried to take the fall for me because my mother didn't get as angry at her. My sister would often say she was to blame for something, even when she wasn't, in order to keep the peace around our house.

My parents finally divorced when I was fifteen. At the time my father told me, "If you do your part, I'll do my part." He meant that he would pay for my college education if I earned good grades and behaved myself. I did my part—I had a 3.8 grade point average when I graduated from Birmingham High School in Van Nuys—but Dad didn't do his. He refused to support me while I was in college. He was still angry with my mother, who had gotten both the house and a good settlement in the divorce. He seemed to blame my mother for his business problems and to blame all three of us for the failure in his personal life. At eighteen, I felt like my dad had deserted me. He had broken his promise to send me to college, and this hurt me in a very big way.

After my parents divorced, my mother dated a lot of men, including her divorce attorney. One day, after my parents' divorce, I came home from school and saw a naked man standing at the top of the stairs. My mother had been sleeping with this guy while my sister and I were at school and apparently didn't expect us home so early.

I was devastated. I was still a very fragile and impressionable young girl. My mother never tried to explain why he was there, nor did she apologize for upsetting us. She never tried to include us, nurture us, or share her feelings with us. She was too involved with herself to think about her kids.

Later, when she had other boyfriends over to the house, she would ask me, "How much will it cost me to have you leave while he's here?" She wanted me out of the house, of course, but she also seemed jealous of the attention her boyfriends gave me. They would flirt with me, a fourteen-year-old kid. It was all in fun and didn't mean anything, but my mom seemed to think it did. I was just a kid looking for attention and God knows I didn't get much attention from her.

Another incident after my parents' divorce occurred when I was sixteen. One night I returned home from a date with my high school boyfriend and went upstairs to get ready for bed. As I walked down the hall, I found two girls, twelve and fourteen, lying on the floor in the extra bedroom with no blankets covering them. My mother had decided to take in two foster children. As I looked at these scared girls on their first night in a strange home, probably too meek even to ask for bedding, I was furious at my mother. I lashed out at her, "You selfish bitch! You just did this for the money." I felt she had no business taking in more kids—she could hardly take care of her own two girls.

I look back in anger and in horror at these events, and I know that they affected me deeply. Now I understand that I'm not responsible for my mother's pain or for her behavior. But I didn't know that growing up. My mother has apologized for all the emotional distress and suffering she has inflicted upon me, either intentionally or unintentionally, over the years. I can accept her apology now, but then, her behavior was devastating.

If you have a bad relationship with your family, I believe it is really important that you heal, find peace, and come to terms with the lack of love or whatever the problem might be. Otherwise you can self-destruct. Children, and even those in their teens and early twenties, are so vulnerable. Self-hate and self-doubt can so easily lead a child to self-destruct. For me, the first thing I developed was an eating disorder: bulimia. Later I became addicted to drugs, and then I became a call girl.

BRIAN HEAD, UTAH, 1976

My First Time: Sex and Skiing

One day, when I was thirteen, I was jumping on a trampoline at Ski World in Los Angeles when John Quildennon, world-class skier and freestyle stud, came over to me and said, "I'm going to get you one day." I responded, probably a little flirtatiously, "Oh no you won't. No way." It's hard to believe that a grown man was really coming on to an adolescent half his age, while she was jumping up and down on a trampoline. But, in Los Angeles, kids grow up fast.

I was a good skier, and after we met I would hang out with John off and on the slopes. He was part of my ski life, and I thought he was really cool. He was practically thirty years old, and I hadn't even reached puberty, but that's what made him seem so cool to me. I was not very developed at thirteen, but by fifteen I had gotten my period and my breasts had begun to grow. That's when John made good on his promise.

We were at Brian Head, Utah, skiing during the day and out at nightclubs in the evening. John must have decided that it was finally time to "get me." And by now I was no longer playing hard to get. During my first sexual experience with this man twice my age, it hurt so much that his penis was not able to fully enter me. It was a disaster. I was crying, bleeding, and very, very scared. I didn't experience anything emotional and certainly not any great passion. I slept with John because I wanted love and attention, and because, like most teenagers, I was anxious to find out what sex was all about.

My best friend at the time, Michelle Girard, was having sex with boys, and I was tired of only hearing about it. I wanted to do it, too. Michelle and I had also experimented with each other sexually when we were fifteen. In bed, during ski trips to Aspen, Utah, and Lake Tahoe, we would kiss and touch each other—kind of playing at sex. Skiing was the main focus of our lives then, but when we weren't thinking about skiing, we were thinking about sex.

I slept with John again a few months later at his house in Tahoe. This time his penis went in all the way and it wasn't such a disaster. John was, after all, a very handsome skier who definitely knew how to use his pole.

Finding My Calling as a Call Girl

Several things happened to me as a young woman that led me to become a call girl. After I graduated from high school, I went to a community college for a while. Then I worked at a couple of nine-to-five office jobs, first as a receptionist in Beverly Hills and later for a financial adviser in Century City. I moved out of my mother's house and lived with my grandmother for a few years. During that time I was dating a guy, Ron, whom I met at a club in Beverly Hills.

Ron was twenty-seven and I was twenty when we met. He was Jewish and an attorney, so to me he seemed like the kind of guy I might end up with. One day after we'd gone out once or twice, he took me back to his house and showed me this huge bag of cocaine he had. He said he wasn't a dealer, and I believed him then. Later, as I got less naive, I wondered why he had so much cocaine if he wasn't a dealer. I did a lot of coke with him, but I kept my habit under control at that time. I still had to hold down my office job.

One night Ron and I were out at Monty's Steak House in Westwood with Ron's seventy-year-old father, a very prominent banker who drove a Rolls-Royce and had a lot of chutzpah. During dinner Ron's father leaned over to me and said, "You could make a thousand a night." I was amazed. I knew he meant that I could make that kind of money by sleeping with men. How else? Later I told my boyfriend what his father had said, and he just laughed. That was one of the first seeds that got planted in my head about being a call girl.

Ron, like his father, was a little kinky. While we were in bed he would want me to pretend that I was making love with another woman. I used to get upset about this fantasy of his and protest, "You're treating me like a hooker." Ironically, it wasn't long after I broke up with him that I became one.

Another strange thing that happened then was that I

met Cathy, a well-known Los Angeles madam. At that time, however, I had no idea who she was. I was working in Beverly Hills, and she saw me one day while I was in a store near my office. She approached me and asked if I would have lunch with her and her husband. They had a business proposition to offer me.

I certainly was interested in ways to make more money. I could barely get by on my salary from my receptionist's job. At lunch Cathy and her husband, Al, talked to me about how I could make a thousand dollars. All I had to do was go see Adnan Khashoggi in Las Vegas. I thought she was crazy at the time. The idea didn't click for me. I wasn't ready to hear about that life yet, especially from Cathy, who seemed so cold and calculating to me. But once again the seed was planted.

Another thing that helped lead me into prostitution was something that happens to a lot of women in this town who ultimately become call girls. We feel used by the men who we date. Guys take us to nightclubs, give us some coke to snort, buy us some new clothes, and take us to dinner or maybe away for the weekend. In return we fuck their brains out, and then it's over. There's nothing else. They just go on to the next beautiful girl for a repeat performance. The men are always the ones in total control. They are the ones with the house in Trousdale and the Porsche in the driveway. The woman just leaves in the morning. And she leaves with nothing—perhaps a few material things, but nothing emotionally.

One of the many guys I dated who belong in this category was a man named Daniel, who had an identical twin brother. Daniel and his twin used to conspire against women, sneaking around pretending that they were the other brother. The other twin was always trying to have sex with me, pretending he was really Daniel. The games these two would play were ridiculous. These twin brothers had all of the Southern California material things—the big house, the Porsche, the coke, and the money. They let me borrow the Porsche and gave me money for shopping. And I fucked for the favors.

On the Westside of Los Angeles—from West Hollywood to Beverly Hills, Brentwood, and the beach—there are a whole lot of young, spoiled, rich guys like those two and women like me who want them. Both the guys and the women think the world owes them everything. They see all the wealth and the materialism and expect that it belongs to them—that they deserve it.

When I was going out with Daniel and others like him, however, I wasn't in the business of being a call girl. My heart kept getting broken. I would go out with a man who would take me to dinner in Beverly Hills. I would become interested in him. He'd ask me to sleep with him on our first date and I would. I would do it with all my heart. I would make love to him and then cuddle up and sleep with him through the night. For him, it was over in the morning. Maybe that's just the difference between men and women. Whatever it was, I got tired of the emptiness. I got tired of waking up with a broken heart.

So it wasn't just one thing that led me into prostitution. It was a series of repeat performances that made me say, "Hey, wait a second, years are going by, I'm an attractive and intelligent woman, yet I'm getting nothing out of relationships but empty promises." I soon had the opportunity to trade those empty promises for some cash.

BEVERLY HILLS, 1984

My First Trick: Ted Field

When I was about twenty-three, I met a girl, Penny, who was working for Madam Alex, the famous Beverly Hills madam. I met Penny at Spago, during a dinner thrown by a big talent agent, Jonathan Axelrod. Penny gave me a line of coke in the bathroom, and we exchanged phone numbers. I was still living with my grandmother and barely making ends meet on the salary from my clerical job. I went over to Penny's place a few days later and was amazed. She lived in a luxury condo on the Wilshire Corridor, drove a Mercedes, had a wardrobe fit for Cinderella, and was only twenty-one years old. I asked her if she had family money or if she had some great job. That's when Penny told me where she got her money.

That night Penny introduced me to the call-girl business and to my first client, Ted Field, a major film producer and heir to the Marshall Field's department stores. Penny had a date to see him and asked if I wanted to come along. If I joined her, she promised she would give me $1,000 of the $2,500 Ted was going to pay her. I was doing a lot of coke and thought, "Why not?" A grand was more than I would make in two weeks at my job.

We got dressed in very sexy outfits—mini-dresses, push-up bras, G-string underwear, beautiful sheer stockings, and high heels—and headed off to meet Ted at an apartment he kept for this purpose. He had left the front door open for us and Penny knew the drill. We took off our dresses and paraded into the bedroom in high heels, just like a couple of hookers. Of course, that was what I was—a first-time hooker—but I felt like I was playing a role. I was a bit uncomfortable, but with Penny there I handled it all right.

Ted was lying on the bed waiting for us. For the next half hour, Penny and I took turns giving him head. She was with him more, because he was her client and because she was, after all, more experienced. That was all there was to it. Thirty minutes later I was $1,000 richer.

Ted was soft-spoken, a gentleman, and to the best of my knowledge, married at the time. Over the years I've heard that he uses call girls regularly, but he only wants women who are in their early twenties. I never saw him again, but for me, Ted Field was an easy way to start out in the business.

EUROPE, 1984

My First Major Client: Adnan Khashoggi

Adnan Khashoggi was my first really big client. I met him through a friend who is now a talent manager in Hollywood, but who at that time, made her money finding female talent for Khashoggi. He was the richest man in the world and had made his fortune in arms trading and various international investments.

On my first trip Khashoggi had four girls, including myself, flown from LAX to Switzerland in a Learjet. We each received a blue Tiffany box with stunning diamond earrings as going-away trinkets. A lavish buffet and Cristal champagne accompanied our Atlantic crossing.

The pilot called my mother for me from the cockpit of the plane. When she answered the phone I said, ''Mom, I'm in the cockpit of the private jet of Adnan Khashoggi on my way to Switzerland." Her first response was, "Oh, can I come?" I reminded her that I was already in the air and basically told her that I was a call girl. She quipped, "Well, you're not doing anything else with your life right now, you might as well be one." So much for parental guidance.

As soon as we arrived in Geneva, we were escorted to a fabulous hotel, the Noga Hilton, where a couple of servants did our bidding as we waited for Adnan to summon us. To pass the time, we shopped, dined, and wandered around for two days with carte blanche to do anything we pleased except buy fine jewelry.

I loved it. We were like a bunch of schoolgirls—jumping on the hotel beds, laughing, and reveling in the excitement of it all. Not everything was fun and games, however. One of the girls, who was really drugged out, claimed that some money was stolen from her, presumably by one of us. Totally frantic, she tried to ransack all of our rooms, looking for the stolen money. Drugs were everywhere on this adventure. Coked out of my mind most of the time, I had begun my serious drug use. One girl was slamming heroin, and though I only did coke, I did every bit Adnan Khashoggi doled out to us, which was about an ounce of coke each. It was sheer madness.

After two days we were flown to Marbella, Spain, where Adnan has an enormous villa on the Mediterranean. When we arrived, I was very impressed by a girl named Ava, who was already there. I wanted to be like her—she was so jet-set, so international, and so glamorous. When I first saw her, this exquisite woman was lying on a couch bed in a luxurious fur coat, with her arms spread wide. She looked like the queen of Sheba. I had no idea then that she, too, was a call girl. This was all such a different world from what I knew. It was the real fast lane.

Despite his legendary wealth and all the rumors about how much Adnan pays his girls, each of us received only $3,000 for our services that week. The amount he pays has been exaggerated by some, but I suppose in a way we did get paid quite a bit more considering all the hotel fees, the restaurant bills, the clothes, and the cocaine we were given, along with everything else we enjoyed. I remember ordering perfume with another one of the girls. We ordered five very expensive bottles of perfume each. I always ordered the most expensive thing on every menu in every restaurant and the best champagne available. We all rationalized that this man was loaded, and we were greedy for whatever he would let us get away with. We were all very young and new to the business.

Of course, there was also plenty of screwing going on. Adnan got his money's worth eventually and slept with all of us at least once over the course of about a week. He only saw one girl a night and would have the one he wanted summoned to his suite.

Sexually, he was a prince and he treated me like a princess. He was more than gentle when I slept with him. I really hate to say anything negative about Adnan, but one of the most powerful men in the world has a penis the size of my thumb. It was definitely the smallest penis I have ever seen in my life.

After that trip to Europe, I saw Adnan several times here in California. We would play in the sheets of the Santa Barbara Biltmore Hotel, and he paid me a thousand dollars for each romp. I consider Adnan Khashoggi my claim to fame as a call girl. If a working girl in this city, or in any other, has not been with Khashoggi, she's simply not top drawer. All of the best girls ended up at his villa in Marbella or somewhere else in Europe with him. It's just the way things are.

Lisa

EUROPE, 1984

Sex on the International Scene

*D*uring the 1984 Olympic Summer Games held in Los
Angeles, I ran an ad to be a tour guide/escort during
the festivities. I figured I could make some money using
my newfound talent as a call girl with the men who were
coming to the city from all over the world. Arthur Schu-
macher, a very prominent Dutch businessman who at one
time had run for prime minister in Holland, answered the
ad. He became my boyfriend/client for the next five years.
Arthur, who was then worth around $60 million, was very
generous to me. He would fly me first-class back and forth
to Holland to see him. We would also meet in the Carib-
bean, at exotic places such as the Golden Tulip on Aruba.
He'd pay me $1,000 a day for as many as thirty days in a
row.

My main duty was to suck him off while he snorted
coke. All day long, coke would be delivered, and I would
suck him over and over again. Then at night there would
be more coke and more sucking. That was what we did
every day. Of course, I was also snorting coke myself right
along with the sex. My drug problem became decidedly
more serious around Arthur than it had ever been.

On one of our trips, Arthur met me at the airport and
noticed that I was wearing a fake Rolex watch. "You can't
wear that knockoff," he protested. "Here, take this one."
He handed me a real Rolex. I later found out that Arthur
was known for paying his girls in watches. Once, when we
were having dinner in London, another girl joined us. I noticed that she was wearing a brand-new gold watch, so I
knew that she, too, had slept with Arthur.

Arthur was also known for the bruises on his ass be-

69

cause he was into being beaten. The other girls he hired apparently took pride in their work. I often saw Arthur with welts and black-and-blue marks on his ass and up and down his thighs. He paid out plenty of gold watches to the girls who were willing to inflict pain upon him, but I wasn't one of them. He once told me that the reason he fell in love with me was that I wouldn't hit him. One time he asked me to burn his feet with a cigarette. He offered me $1,000 for the act, so I really attempted to do it, but I couldn't hurt him. It's just not in me.

Despite, or perhaps because of, the fact that I wouldn't beat him, Arthur asked me to marry him. He wanted me to have his baby. He told me that he was Jewish, but since he was uncircumcised I didn't believe him. He claimed that it was very important to him to marry a Jewish girl and have a baby. He insisted, however, that the child be a Dutch citizen.

When I told him that I didn't want to marry him, Arthur offered me $250,000 to have his baby and leave the child with him in Holland. I was outraged. "If you want that kind of service, don't ask a Jewish girl," I told him. "I'm not leaving my baby anywhere for any amount of money."

Around this time, Arthur's world started to unravel. Over the years, he had funneled millions out of Holland and into Switzerland to avoid his country's high taxes. He was finally caught smuggling $400,000 back into Holland from his Swiss account. The money was confiscated. This was the beginning of his demise. Around this time he would take me out to dinner and would have two guns on the center console of his Jaguar. He claimed that the whole country was out to get him. A short time later he shot up the business window of a partner who hadn't repaid a $100,000 loan. Another time I had to hide under a restaurant table to avoid a potential gun battle between Arthur and another guy. I believe it was the cocaine, more than anything, that sent him over the edge. Arthur eventually lost his visa and was unable to travel to the U.S. Before that, however, he sent me packing. My last trip paid for by Arthur was a one-way return ticket to the U.S. in coach class.

Arthur ended his own life, shooting himself in the mouth. At the time he died, he still had money but was no longer worth $60 million. His estate was left in equal parts to his brother, to a child he eventually had (though not with me), and to Faye Dunaway. Arthur had a strange obsession with Faye Dunaway. He wanted to marry her also and have children with her. Once he jumped up onstage in London where she was performing, screaming, "I love you, Faye Dunaway. You've got to marry me." He was hauled off by security guards.

Arthur was a man who once ran for prime minister of a nation, who also happened to be a major coke addict and who loved my blow jobs. Life can be very strange, indeed.

VENICE, 1985

Three Is Not a Crowd with Dennis Hopper

Some really big deals are consummated during the Wednesday night Alcoholics Anonymous meetings in Los Angeles, not to mention a goodly share of dating and mating as well. I met Dennis Hopper at an AA meeting. He's a recovering drug addict and alcoholic who has been clean and sober for over ten years. He is married now, but when

I knew him he was very available, especially when it came to me and my friend Melinda.

Melinda, a call-girl friend of mine, was hanging out at my apartment one day. We had nothing to do, so we decided to go "dialing for dollars"—that's what we call drumming up business in the prostitution trade. It's similar to the cold calls that stock or real estate brokers make. A lot of professional call girls go into real estate as a second career—it's a natural transition.

We called Dennis Hopper that day, and he turned out to be a ready customer. It was a lovely afternoon of primal three-way sex. Melinda and I did each other and he was like a big bear on the loose, an insatiable hungry animal that devours its prey.

There are no boundaries with Dennis—he's sweet, kinky, and very animalistic. Afterward he took me and Melinda out to a very chic lunch at Chaya in Venice. We were all pretty hungry after the sexual workout.

BEL AIR, 1986

Berry Gordy Was the Real Thing

I was involved with Arthur on and off for five years. During the off periods, I usually worked for Madam Alex. I had nothing but the highest regard for Alex. She is one woman who knew how to make money. Unfortunately, her life seemed so unhappy. She had diabetes and she abused coke, which made her health even worse. She was unmarried and just sat around all day at home in a big granny dress making calls. She loved her phone—it was her line to money.

One of the early clients Madam Alex introduced me to was Berry Gordy, Mr. Motown himself. He was also one of my favorite clients. He was a wonderful, sweet guy with a generous manner who made me feel very loved, even though I was just a working girl. We met at a strange place, the Holiday Inn in Bel Air on North Church Lane off Sunset Boulevard, right off the San Diego Freeway. It's a big, round, phallic-looking hotel that attracts mostly tourists because it's convenient to both the homes of the stars and Universal Studios.

I loved seeing Berry because he made me feel so comfortable and wanted. To me, Berry Gordy is a quality human being. He wanted straight sex—nothing kinky—and paid $500 for about an hour. I was happy to accommodate this kind and easygoing man who had revolutionized music around the world.

BEVERLY HILLS, 1986

Picked by the Prince

The call-girl circuit in Los Angeles is filled with women who all know each other and have a lot in common—for one thing, the same men. One way we get to know each other is through jobs where a guy wants several girls at a time and, of course, the ever-popular threesomes. Another way we meet is when a rich Arabian royal orders a roomful of girls.

On one of these multiple-girl jobs, Madam Alex asked

me to go see Prince Fahad of Saudi Arabia, who at the time was seventeen years old. There was an entire squadron of local female talent at the Beverly Hilton for the young stud to choose from. I arrived to find him skateboarding on the marble floors of his hotel suite, giving us all the once-over. I was nervous, so I started skateboarding around the marble floor, too. Of course, he picked me over the rest. Hooking is often similar to a Hollywood casting call where only one girl gets the part, and it's always the one who stands out in some way.

We went to his bedroom and the kid wasted no time in making his moves. He was very thin, good-looking, tall, and broad-shouldered. Mostly, however, he was very well endowed. If nothing else, this prince was the prince of penis. I stared at him, mesmerized by his huge dick.

As a call girl I'm not particularly fond of big penises. I just want the guy to enter me and get off, not work me over like this kid did. With his big cock so far inside me, I began to feel more excited—and the last thing I want is to get involved. It was too much like having sex with a boy-friend. The purpose of being in the business for me was to avoid any emotional connection.

Finally, after an hour he'd had enough. I was glad that he had picked me but also was glad to get out. I got paid $800 for the job, but with the workout he gave me, it should have been even more.

BEVERLY HILLS, 1986

The Hollywood Connection

I saw a lot of the big Hollywood players during my career. A well-known producer, whom I'll call Alan Smithee, is a major player when it comes to the call-girl trade. Many of my friends were seeing Alan and seeing him often. I heard that he would spend $2,000 to have a girl defecate on him. I thought it was very strange but had learned in my time as a Hollywood call girl that sometimes the most powerful men were the sickest.

When I met Alan myself, I was grateful that the experience was a little different from the kind of thing I'd heard about. Not that it was a great experience. When I went up to his house, he wanted to lie in bed, smoke cocaine cigarettes, and watch everything he had produced in a very full lifetime in Hollywood. I wasn't interested.

When I'm on cocaine, I can't give anybody a lot of attention and that's what Alan wanted. Coke is a miserable drug for me. It makes me unhappy, paranoid, and uncomfortable in my skin. Coke was the reason why Alan and I had trouble with one another. In the state I was in, I just couldn't play all of his games and follow the routine the way he wanted it done.

Despite my problem with his egocentric personality, I introduced Alan to a girlfriend of mine, Rachel, who hit it off with him. Rachel was from Orange County, and she was more dazzled by all of the Hollywood stuff. Alan just loves it when someone is impressed by his greatness.

Rachel was definitely able to fawn all over him. I don't know, however, if she was able to shit all over him—but I'm sure he wanted her to.

BEVERLY HILLS, 1986

A Regular Threesome

Bisexuality is a big part of the call-girl business. A good call girl has to be bisexual or at least willing to partake

75

in homosexual activity, or her career will be severely limited. Often a guy will want a call girl to do his girlfriend while he watches, his hand groping his erection. At least 25 percent of the time a call girl's job is to act out some male fantasy that involves two women.

A friend introduced me to a big-shot agent at International Creative Management (ICM) named Seth. Seth was living on Roxbury Drive in Beverly Hills at the time with his girlfriend Ellen, a former Miss USA. She was stunningly beautiful, with honey-colored skin, long brown hair, and big flashing eyes. Ellen was also very beautiful on the inside. She was kind, sweet, and soft-spoken, and had a wonderful attitude toward life and other people.

Seth hired me regularly for threesomes with him and Ellen. I saw them almost once a week for about six months. During the call, Ellen and I would make love to each other, and he would have sex with each of us. She was the only woman I ever really enjoyed having sex with.

Seth, on the other hand, was a two-timing prick. He would arrange to see me behind Ellen's back. He was never mean to me or mean to Ellen in front of me, but I could tell that she was miserably unhappy with him. He was very controlling and he treated her like a call girl, even though he always referred to her as his girlfriend.

I always felt that Ellen was just like me. What is the difference between a call girl and a girlfriend who is treated like one? Actually, especially during those threesomes, I suspected that Ellen might have been a call girl at some point in her life. She certainly had the skill.

BEVERLY HILLS, 1987

Alexander Godunov: Addicted to Hookers

I was sent by Madam Alex to another Alex, Alexander Godunov. It was a one-hour call for $500. I was surprised that this man had the audacity to call a hooker. He was living at the time with a woman I admire, actress Jackie Bisset, in her house at the top of Coldwater Canyon in Beverly Hills.

When I first met Godunov, he was drunk, and I had my period. He wanted to eat me, and it didn't matter to him that I was bleeding. When I saw him with my blood all over his face I was grossed out. Clearly, he was more open-minded and adventurous than I was at that point in my life.

Godunov was a talented but tortured man. He was a recovering alcoholic who was unable to recover, and he eventually killed himself. He became a regular client of mine and would often caution me about the dangers of alcohol and drugs. He'd warn me as I was taking a drink, "Lisa, you've got to stop that." Unfortunately, he didn't take his own advice and kept drinking.

Whenever we had sex in Jackie Bisset's bed, Alexander was completely hammered, drunk out of his mind. He would be too wasted to get hard so he usually just ate my pussy. I couldn't understand why he needed me, a twenty-six-year-old hooker, when he had such a beautiful and talented girlfriend. To me, Jackie Bisset was everything I thought a man would want in a woman. Why did he need to call hookers? I never found the answer. Maybe for him it was an addiction, just like the alcohol.

Eventually Alexander moved from Jackie's house to an apartment in West Hollywood. I saw him again after he moved, and he wanted to know if I had any girlfriends. Of course I did. I gave him some numbers and told him to call them. He called plenty of my friends before he died.

The Business in the Big Apple

After my Dutch boyfriend/client Arthur and I broke up for the last time, on my way back from Europe I stopped in New York to visit a girlfriend. This friend was also a call girl and I thought I would do a client or two with her while I was there. I found out, however, that she was actually working in a brothel.

There were several girls who worked out of this apartment/brothel, which was run by a very vivacious, red-headed Jewish madam. This madam would sit in the kitchen area, do the paperwork, and set up the calls while the girls serviced the clients in the bedrooms or hung out in the living room, waiting for clients to arrive. When I showed up, the madam was very excited. She called up all of her regular clients and told them that "new talent" was available—me.

I saw five clients a day because everyone who came in wanted to see me. It was way too many for me. I was used to only one client a day back in L.A. By the second or third day, I couldn't take it anymore. I had to quit. The money also wasn't what I had become accustomed to. This madam took 50 percent instead of the standard 40 percent that L.A. madams took. The clients only paid $200 or $300—rather than the going rate of $300 to $500 in L.A.—which meant I only cleared about $100 to $150 a trick.

I left the brothel, but I didn't leave New York right away. The night I quit, I went out to a nightclub and met a guy, Jeffrey, a married man who worked at a brokerage firm. Jeffrey instantly developed a big crush on me and offered me a job if I stayed in New York. "Why not?" I thought. It would be a change and possibly fun.

Jeffrey was only twenty-seven years old but was already a partner at his brokerage firm. He came from money so I figured he had bought into the company. He leased me a furnished apartment and I went to work on Wall Street as an executive secretary for Jeffrey. I worked there for seven months until Jeffrey had me fired because I slept with somebody else in the firm. It made me really angry. He was married, of course, but he expected me to be loyal to him.

By then, I had had it with the Big Apple anyway. I was ready to return to the better climate and the higher-paying clients in L.A.

WEST VIRGINIA, 1989

Time-Out with Steven Tyler

My friend Liza arranged for me to meet Steven Tyler by flying me to West Virginia where Aerosmith was giving a concert. This wasn't really a job—it was more for fun. Michelle Girard, my friend from high school, who was now a world class freestyle skier, went with me. Michelle had never been a call girl, but she was a big Aerosmith fan.

Tyler ended up liking Michelle better than me. She was

petite, with an athlete's body. She was the right size for this rocker, who felt I was a little too tall for him.

Michelle and I had a fabulous time in West Virginia. We had backstage passes and deluxe hotel accommodations. Since we weren't getting paid anything except our expenses, we even went into the hotel boutique and signed for about $800 in jewelry. We got in trouble for that, however. Tyler may be a rock star, but he's a cheap rock star.

Steven Tyler was married at the time and off drugs. His wife was also off drugs and had apparently helped him get into recovery. We saw him both nights we were in town. He slept with both of us and was particularly into the oral sex.

I look upon blow jobs as my little revenge on men. Through oral sex, with just a little effort I can make the money and have the control and the luxury that a man has in life. Of course, I doubt that women who aren't in the business think of it the same way.

After our fun in West Virginia, Michelle and I flew back to L.A. where she returned to her skiing world and I returned to my business.

BEVERLY HILLS, 1989

Warren Beatty Loves Phone Sex

I became friends with a woman, Denise Beaumont, who was close friends with the well-known, debauched producer Alan Smithee. Denise had married a rich man, Bob Beaumont, and had become the biggest socialite party girl on the L.A. circuit. Denise was written up in every social column for years, and she knew everybody.

Denise introduced me to Alan Smithee's friend, actor Warren Beatty, on the phone. She said to me one day, "I just want you to call up Warren and talk to him." Thinking it might lead to some work, or at least to some fun, I called up Warren Beatty as Denise had suggested. It turned out to be a big letdown. All Warren wanted was to talk sexy on the phone. That was it. I got bored after a while and hung up. He had my number, however, so he called me a few times after that. He would go on and on with questions like, "Tell me what you look like." Or, "How's your hair?" And, "Do you polish your toenails?" There wasn't even any sick stuff—just a bunch of boring, drag-on telephone talk.

Though he would ask me to come over and play during these calls, I got the definite feeling that he didn't care if I came over or not. He just rambled on like a lonely, bored, and horny guy. I sure hope that his marriage to Annette Bening is going okay. Maybe she should keep her eye on the phone bills, however.

HOLLYWOOD, 1989

Implants for Shep Gordon

Shep Gordon, a powerful man in the music industry, was a call girl's dream. The third time I saw him, I happened to look in the mirror at my breasts and complained that I would love to have them done. He turned to me and said, "No problem." Shep considered new breasts for me an investment in his own pleasure.

At his office later that week, Shep handed me an envelope with $2,500 in traveler's checks. He told me to go see a breast doctor and to come back and show him the results the minute they were done. Later that night I went to the American Music Awards with a girlfriend, using tickets Shep had also given me. He was just a very loving and generous guy and I was proud to have breast implants put in for him.

Shep became a good client of mine, like a friend, and I saw him for several years. He had an Asian chef who would make us dinner at the house. We would dine and then have sex. He was an absolute doll and was totally conventional and normal, sexually speaking. Actually he was the kind of man I would have loved to marry.

HOLLYWOOD, 1990

Hitting Bottom

No matter what career you are in, a bad drug habit can really bring you down to your lowest point. Since drugs and prostitution are so intertwined, a lot of high-class call girls end up at some point living in cheap hotels and working for $100 a trick just so they can support their drug habit. That's what happened to me.

As my drug problem escalated, I ended up renting a room in a Hollywood hotel for $30 a night so I would be closer to my drug dealers. I was smoking rock cocaine then, which cost me $20 a rock. Every day I'd have to drag my-self out of bed to find a trick or two to pay for food, the hotel room, and the next night's fix. It was a miserable time.

During this period I also had one of the most traumatic experiences of my life. I was trying to score some drugs at five o'clock one morning when I was grabbed by two black guys and pulled into their car. I managed to kick the front windshield out of the car and jump out onto the street, landing on my knees and hurting them pretty badly. I waved down another car for help, and it turned out to be the backup car for the first two guys. Three more guys, friends of the jerks from whom I had just escaped, were in this car. They pulled me in with them. One of them put a gun to my head and said, "White bitch, we're going to kill your white ass." They were members of the Crips, a big L.A. gang.

They took me to a trailer somewhere in the Valley, beat me up, punched me in the head, and took turns raping me. I can't believe I lived. By noon the next day, all of them, except one, had left the trailer. Fortunately, the property manager, demanding the rent, pounded on the door and finally pushed it open. I seized the opportunity, jumped out of the trailer, and ran for my life.

I never went to therapy or sought any help after being raped by those gang members. I thought, I guess, that I could handle it because I was a call girl at the time it hap-pened. I think if something like that happened to my younger sister, who is a married schoolteacher, it would be far more traumatic. I wouldn't want to see anyone I love go through the shit I've been through. Yet I kept putting myself through it until I finally got sober.

HAWAII, 1990

In the Air with Kareem Abdul-Jabbar

*I*f you ever wondered whether or not a call girl can get involved in a relationship with a client—aside from in the fantasy movie *Pretty Woman*—the answer is yes. I started dating a man I had first met as a client, Jeff, a Jewish guy who was a cameraman for TV and films. He was a nice guy with a nice career and was raising his eleven-year-old daughter by himself following the tragic suicide of his wife.

I moved in with Jeff after I had been off drugs for only a month, which is not very much time for an addict to really trust herself or to know how she really feels. I wanted the security, however, so I took the leap. It wasn't fair to Jeff or to me, since I wasn't ready for a relationship.

Shortly after we got together, Jeff took me on a vacation to Hawaii. Wanting to impress me, he bought first-class tickets. In the first-class cabin with us that trip was the king of the court, Kareem Abdul-Jabbar. Kareem, who was a resident of Hawaii, and I flirted with each other behind Jeff's back and exchanged numbers. Here I was, sober for a month, trying to turn my life around, living with a great guy but a few minutes in the air in first class and I was giving Kareem my number. I didn't know myself then like I know myself today. I was still really fucked up. Of course, it didn't end there.

The next thing I knew, Kareem was over at our hotel and he and I were sneaking off for lunch together. He kissed me passionately and wanted me to sleep with him. We drove around the island for about an hour and he used his formidable sex appeal to try to wear me down, but I didn't sleep with him. Instead, I ran into another guy I had known back in L.A., who I went off with. I abandoned my boyfriend, Jeff, who had taken me to Hawaii in the first place.

The guy from L.A. ended up going back to his girlfriend, Jeff went home, and I had nobody. I definitely deserved what I got. The worst part is that I don't know why I did any of it. I don't know why I went after Kareem, why I chased the other guy, and why I left poor Jeff in the lurch.

BEVERLY HILLS, 1991

A Freebie for Stallone

I was always a big fan of Sly Stallone. I loved his movies. I had a pal, Joey Pinto, a starstruck, wanna-be type of guy who knew Sly. One night Joey told me that he and I were invited to Stallone's house. Joey said he had told Sly that I was a call girl and that I would give Sly head for a fee. I went with Joey on the understanding that Stallone knew I was a pro and wasn't there as some starstruck bimbo ready and willing to do whatever for free. I was no sooner in the door than I went upstairs with Stallone.

There I was in his incredible home, in the bedroom of one of the world's richest movie stars, giving him head. It wasn't difficult—I sucked, he came, and then I left. He was rushed because he had a date with another girl that night and was late. Worse than his abruptness, however, was the fact that Stallone never paid me. I thought, "This is lovely. How used can a person feel? How taken advantage of?" It all had happened because my starstruck friend Joey wanted to get closer to Stallone by providing him with a call girl. I felt very stupid for letting myself be used by this wanna-be. Not getting paid really makes me feel used. I think I'll skip the next few Stallone movies—not that he'll go broke over it.

Ivan and Heidi: Not the Perfect Couple

The only encounter I ever had with the infamous Hollywood Madam, Heidi Fleiss, was when I met her with her boyfriend, Ivan Nagy, at the Roxbury nightclub. They were with another girl I knew, Chauncey, who died some time later from a drug-related suicide. I had met Chauncey in AA. We had both been in the program for several years and she became a friend of mine. Chauncey was bisexual, and I had heard that Heidi had a regular thing with her.

Ivan Nagy, Heidi's boyfriend at the time, is a very manipulative man with a very definite agenda. He is arrogant, aggressive, and persuasive. If he wants a girl to go to bed with him, he'll find a way to make it happen. There is no saying no to him.

One time Ivan invited me over to his house. We were in his den and he was at his desk when all of a sudden he showed me a picture of Heidi. In the photo she was naked and lying on her back. I thought to myself, "What a piece of shit this guy is. What kind of a man would degrade his girlfriend this way?" In my opinion, Nagy displayed his own weakness and insecurity by showing me that photo. He showed me his black heart.

Next he had the audacity to say to me, "I could make

you the next Heidi Fleiss, you know." I assumed he meant professionally, not personally, but maybe he thought I had a thing for him and that's why he was showing me the photo. All I could think was, "Oh please, don't do me any favors. I don't want to be the next Heidi Fleiss in any form."

Being a madam is like being a surrogate mother to a lot of needy women. There's a great deal of pressure. Someone is always miserable and the madam has to listen to all the problems. Add to that the drug addictions of many of the call girls and the problems those addictions cause. Believe me, being a madam is one position that I was not applying for. I got out of there, and that was the last I saw of Ivan Nagy.

LOS ANGELES, 1996

Boyfriend Blues

A lot of people don't realize that call girls have boy-friends just like everyone else. And they're not all guys like Ivan Nagy, though I've had my share of jerks. Of course, the guys I've been with had to be pretty open-minded to accept what I did for a living. I always told them, "I never cheated on you other than my business." I always explained to a boyfriend that being with a client is not at all the same as being with a lover. First, there's no emotional connection with the client. It's just a business transaction. Second, the sex is about giving the man pleasure, not about giving me pleasure. I didn't have orgasms with clients—though I often faked them—when I had a boyfriend in my life. My boyfriend was always the one who had the responsibility to see that I was satisfied sexually.

Of course, I have to question how much a guy really loved me if he was able to handle my being a call girl. The last call I got from Madam Alex was for a job at the Four Seasons Hotel with one of her major Japanese clients, in town on a business trip. It was a $1,500 job. I would get 60 percent, which came to $900, and I really needed the money. Asian clients, as a rule, are very easy. They often have small penises and are not a lot of work.

I never made it to the Four Seasons for that call. I had told my boyfriend at the time that I didn't work as a call girl any more, and when he found out about this job, he was furious. He tied me to a chair with nylon stockings around my hands and ankles to stop me from going. I felt terrible because I had promised Alex that I wouldn't let her down. But there I was, imprisoned in my own apartment by my crazy jealous boyfriend.

He was really nuts about my working because his mother and his sisters had both been hookers. Despite how upset I was at losing that $900 job, I understood his jealousy. I, too, am jealous and possessive. If I found out that one of my boyfriends put his penis in another woman, I would castrate him. A year and a half ago, when I was still working, my boyfriend at the time told me, "I'm gonna go be a gigolo because you're a call girl." I wigged. "Not on your life," I told him. I have what you might call a double standard because it seems different to me. A guy has to be aroused to get his penis hard and stick it in a woman. I didn't have to feel a thing to do what I did.

Since I've been in this business, I haven't attracted the kind of guy I would be likely to want to marry. The boyfriends I've picked haven't been very successful or together—usually they need my help financially. Because of my profession, I haven't really been able to be receptive to the kind of guy who wants to get married and have kids. I have what it takes to be a married woman, but what was I going to tell a nice normal guy—"Hi, I'm a hooker"?

Dangers and Disorders

Drugs are a very well-known problem for prostitutes, but there are other dangers common to the profession as well. A less talked-about but very prevalent problem that women in my business have is eating disorders. Staying thin is necessary to attract clients and we call girls don't always watch our weight in the healthiest ways. I myself have been bulimic for many years. It started when I was a teenager and only in recent years have I gotten it under control. I know many other call girls who have the same problem. We used to go out to lunch together and then throw up our food after lunch.

Part of getting sober and getting my life together has been coming to terms with how I feel about food. I'm finally at peace with it. Now I can eat lunch without thinking about throwing it up afterward. It's a wonderful feeling.

At one point, when I was traveling all over and living the high life, my father wanted to know where I was getting all my money. So I told him the truth—that I was a call girl. He's a very grounded guy and didn't blow up or anything. He just warned me, "I hope you make enough money to retain an attorney." He also wanted to know if I was practicing safe sex.

Even when I was a heavy drug user, I was careful about making sure I had protection on a job. I always insisted on it. I even made the guys use condoms for oral sex. After a while I wouldn't let clients eat me, nor would I let them kiss me. These precautions might have limited me in the business but I wasn't willing to take the risk of contracting AIDS or other sexually transmitted diseases like gonorrhea. With my father's help, I always kept up payments on my health insurance and got regular checkups.

As far as my father's warning about the legal problems I could run into as a call girl, that was another story. I went to jail twice: once in 1990 for a short time for possession of cocaine and then later for six months for violation of my probation. I've finally gotten all of my legal problems cleared up, thank God. Jail is one place I don't want to be ever again. You never realize how wonderful freedom is until it is taken away from you.

LOS ANGELES, 1996

Life Lessons

As an adult, at thirty-five years of age, I now realize what problems I faced as a child, but I don't know if I would have turned out differently had I not had those problems with my parents. My younger sister, who grew up in the same environment, is happily married and raising a beautiful child today. As kids, I was the emotional one, the one who needed the most attention. She was less outgoing as a child than I was, and she didn't seem to need the same amount of attention.

I realize now that my sister became the more balanced and the less needy person because she had to march to her own drummer. She had to find her own happiness, and in so doing, she found out who she really was. My sister did not have to rely on the "comfort of strangers" or on family to give her an approval rating all the time, to tell her how terrific she was, how beautiful, how thin, how perfect.

My sister's life took a very different route from mine. She went to college, earned her master's degree, and became a teacher. She has been with her husband since she was twenty, and they struggled together through school. She didn't have a free ride.

As much as I admire and respect my sister, I'm not sure that I would want to trade places with her. I have to admit that I'm a different person. I was once unable to live a simple life. I love the big lifestyle, the excitement, the glamour, and I always have. I probably always will.

My mother and I are pretty good friends today. I have been working on healing our relationship, and finally my mother has become a close friend of mine. This woman I despised as a child for her obsessive and selfish behavior is important in my life today. I know that for me to heal, it's important that our relationship heal, and I'm proud to say that it has.

I've been out of the prostitution business now for a year and a half. It's hard to leave because the business never goes away. Opportunities come along when old friends and clients turn up. Whenever a call girl tells me she is completely out of the business, I'm never sure it's true.

Today my goal is to stay clean and healthy, off drugs, and out of rehabs, and to make a new life for myself. I want a career. I want to find the right man, get married, and have babies. I want to love my mother and my father and my sister—to forgive, forget, and move on. I know it's not too late for me. I also know I need to face the past truthfully and overcome the insecurity, the greed, and the drug-induced irrationality that made me search for an easy road to glamour and the high life.

I don't consider myself a victim. I made my own choices and I have to take responsibility for them. I want to learn from my past and really understand who I am now, as an adult. I'd like to find a new way to fit into this "man's world"—without getting even by selling my body. I'd like to be able to help other women—young, attractive women—choose a healthier lifestyle than the one I chose for so many years. I'm grateful for every new opportunity to turn things around; to be a winner, not a loser; and most importantly, to be a productive member of society.

PART TWO

Children
of the
Night

Hollywood is not just the glamorous movie capital of the world, with sex for sale at five-star hotels and producers' mansions. It is also a place where hundreds of children walk the streets at night—children who have been abandoned and neglected by their parents; emotionally distraught children on the run from the chaos of their dysfunctional families; children looking for love, affection, drugs, money, or all of the above. These lost children roam the streets of Hollywood night after night, doing what they have to do to survive. The girls may sometimes find an older man to be their sugar daddy. More often they find a pimp.

While Michelle and Lisa consciously chose to sell themselves to make money, Sophie and Jewel, like other lost children of the night, stumbled into prostitution, trying to fill a deep, empty hole inside themselves, trying to find something to replace their lost innocence and lost childhoods.

Sophie was 15 when her family fell apart and she sought solace and security from other party girls, older men, prostitutes, and drug addicts. She was even younger, 12, when she was first seduced by a much older member of a famous band, and 13 when she first learned to make money by selling her body. Jewel was not quite as young when her close-knit family disintergrated around her—she was 19 and a student at Harvard University. Though Jewel's mind may have been filled with book knowledge, at the time of her mother's nervous breakdown she knew very little about how to take care of herself emotionally. Eventually abandoned by both parents and a cruel stepmother, Jewel sought family with porno stars, pimps, and prostitutes—people as desperate for some sort of love and acceptance as she was.

Sophie and Jewel, like Michelle and Lisa, have also had sexual encounters with celebrities and powerful men in Hollywood. Their stories, however, present a more obviously harrowing picture than Michelle's and Lisa's of what happens to young women caught up in that life. Sophie takes us beyond cocaine into the frighteningly dangerous world of heroin addiction. Jewel leads us away from Beverly Hills into the sleazy domain of porno filmmaking and lower-class hooking. Though not quite down at the $50-a-shot level of Hugh Grant's Hollywood prostitute, Divine Brown, Jewel still sold herself for far less than the call girls we've met so far, who lived on the other side of the tracks.

As you read Sophie's and Jewel's stories, hundreds of other lonely, lost, frightened young girls with big chips on their shoulders and bad attitudes are tonight wandering the streets, the bars, the cheap hotels, and the shooting galleries of Hollywood. These stories are dedicated to those other children of the night, many of whom may never make it home.

Sophie

HEIGHT:	*5'8"*
HAIR:	*Blond*
EYES:	*Green*
WEIGHT:	*120*
PROFESSION:	*Graphic artist; mother*
HOBBIES:	*Painting and sculpture*
EDUCATION:	*Dropped out of high school*
FIRST SEXUAL EXPERIENCE:	*At age 11 in a seedy hotel with a guy I don't remember*
GOALS AND DESIRES:	*To continue being self-sufficient and providing the healthiest environment for my kids*
SEXUAL FANTASY:	*I wish I had one*
DRUGS:	*Pot, Bacardi 151, angel dust, acid, Quaaludes, yellow jackets, Placidyl, cocaine, heroin, and anything else I could get my hands on*
HAPPIEST MEMORY:	*When my kids were born*
WORST EXPERIENCE:	*Having my face smashed by an angry drug dealer*
SEX PARTNERS:	*Dennis Wilson, Adnan Khashoggi, Scott Baio, Anthony Delon, Saudi princes, Jerry Buss, Gabe Kaplan, Jack Nicholson*

Growing Up Too Soon

People who know me today have no idea what I went through as a teenager. Sometimes, as I tell my story, it's even hard for me to imagine that I'm the same person. I'm also amazed—and grateful—that I'm still alive today.

My mother and father divorced when I was two and my father moved to another state. A few years later my mother married again, this time to an older businessman who adored her and who gave her the freedom she never had in those early years, as a single mother saddled with two kids. After they were married, we moved to an upper-middle-class neighborhood in the Hollywood Hills.

My new stepfather, George, assumed most of the responsibility for raising me, my brother, and my stepsister. My mother enrolled in college, eventually working on her Ph.D., and traveled a lot doing research. She was a very free-spirited, 1970s hippie type. George, even though he was a straight-laced corporate man, thought that Mom was really cool. They had this room called "the Groovy Room" that they painted in psychedelic colors, lit with strobe lights, and furnished with a water bed. When we were little, my brother and I would go into the Groovy Room, turn on the strobe lights, and jump up and down on the water bed.

We also had a music room, with a harp, a piano, and several other instruments. My stepfather was very cultivated, and we'd listen to opera every Sunday while we cleaned the house.

My mom and my stepdad used to keep marijuana and hashish in the music room. When they would smoke pot I thought, "This stinks. It's disgusting." But not much later, when I was only in the second grade, I showed my parents' stash to some friends of mine who were in the sixth grade. They taught me how to roll a joint, and that's when I started doing drugs. I didn't enjoy pot that much at first—it made me hungry—but I believed that I was very cool.

I was really into being cool. I always wanted to do what others, in particular older friends, would think was cool. It was cool to smoke pot. It was cool to hitchhike. It was cool to panhandle to get money to buy Quaaludes. If I thought it was cool, I would do it.

I was eleven when I first had sex. A group of us, most of the kids older than me, used to hang out at a skating rink in the San Fernando Valley. The girls would tease me because I was still a virgin. Naturally I wanted to be cool, so I went with a bunch of them to this terrible dive-type hotel in the Valley and had sex for the first time with some guy. I was very high and don't remember much about it except that I wasn't alone with the boy. The whole crowd was there.

My mother didn't believe in setting boundaries or disciplining me. I was allowed to use bad language, stay out as late as I wanted, and dress however I chose. It was more like I was renting a room, rather than being a child, in that house.

The older crowd I hung out with also frequented a teen-age nightclub in the Valley, the Sugar Shack. One night a couple friends of mine took me to another club, over the hill in Hollywood. This was where I first met Scotty Wilson, the son of the Beach Boys drummer, Dennis Wilson.

Scotty and I became boyfriend and girlfriend, but in truth we were more like partners in crime. We partied, did drugs, hitchhiked around town, robbed houses, and stole cars. We were arrested several times. My mother wasn't usually around, so my stepfather would bail me out of jail. By the third time he had had it with me and let me stay in Juvenile Hall a week before he brought me home.

HOLLYWOOD, 1977

This Beach Boy Was a Real Bastard

I first met Scotty's dad, Dennis Wilson, the day Scotty and I went to a Beach Boys concert at the Universal Amphitheatre. Scotty and his dad picked me up in his dad's black Rolls-Royce Corniche convertible. The top was down when they pulled into my driveway. To a twelve-year-old brat, who was so into what was cool, this whole night was the coolest. As I sat in the amphitheatre during the concert, I looked up at Dennis Wilson onstage and thought, "Oh my God, he's so cute." I instantly developed a crush on him, the kind teenagers always have on performers.

At the time Dennis Wilson was living with Christine McVie of Fleetwood Mac. I would often go with Scotty up to her house on Lindacrest Drive in Beverly Hills. Mick Fleetwood was usually there and so was Stevie Nicks. Everyone would get high, play music, and sing. Scotty and I would run around the house trying to find out where the

103

drugs were hidden. Though the adults were always doing drugs, Christine would never let Scotty and me partake.

One day I was at the house when Stevie Nicks came over. She pulled up her top and said to the crowd, "Look, everybody, I've got new breasts." There they were—silicone's finest. It was the first I had ever heard of boob jobs.

After I'd been hanging out with Scotty for a while, Dennis Wilson started to pay a lot of attention to me. He used to say, "Come on, Sophie, let's go shopping." We'd jump into his Corniche and he'd drive us to a store called Maxfield's in Beverly Hills. He bought me anything I wanted. Later I learned that it was Christine McVie who was buying me anything I wanted, because Dennis was charging everything to her card.

Dennis and I started to get closer. One night when I was over at the house with Scotty, Dennis came in and announced that my stepfather had called. He wanted me to come home right away. Dennis told us he had promised my stepdad that he would bring me home. Scotty wanted to come along for the ride, but Dennis said no—he had to head somewhere else right after dropping me off.

I had such a crush on Dennis that I would get knots in my stomach whenever I was alone with him. As we drove off into the night, he turned to me and said, "I made that up about your stepfather calling. You don't have to go right home. I want to spend some time alone with you. I want to take you to a special place, a place that will be our special place."

We drove to a cute little house off Laurel Canyon on Yucca Terrace. The house was empty except for a mattress on the floor in one of the bedrooms. Dennis gave me a Quaalude, we did some coke, and, as usual, he was drinking. He used to drink rum and orange juice all the time. He would pour out half the orange juice from a container and fill it back up with rum. We called it his jug. He had it with him all the time, regularly taking swigs from it.

We sat down together on the mattress and Dennis poured his drunken heart out to me. He told me he'd never felt this way about a girl before. He said that he wanted to be with me badly. I was so in awe of this man that I didn't resist. Besides, I thought I was in love with him, that this was a dream come true. At twelve years old I believed this was the best thing that could ever happen to me.

Our affair lasted throughout that entire summer and continued on after school started in the fall. We would sneak off to be alone together in all sorts of places. Dennis would come over to my house in the middle of the night and tap on my window with a twig or a stone. I'd sneak out of the house to meet him. Often he'd want to know if there was any food in the house, and I'd have to sneak back into the kitchen to make him a plate of food. Then we'd usually drive off and go buy drugs. I was so cool that of course I knew all the best dealers around.

I felt a little guilty about Scotty, who at first didn't know what was going on. I rationalized the situation in my mind by believing what Dennis had told me, that he wasn't Scotty's real father. Somehow, in my young, infatuated mind, I believed if that was true, it was okay for me to be sleeping with Dennis.

Scotty wasn't stupid, however, and he soon suspected that something was going on. One night he hid in the bushes surrounding my house and saw his father pick me up. When I returned home from my date with Dennis, Scotty was still there waiting for me. As Dennis drove off, Scotty followed me into my house, yelling and crying hysterically. In the kitchen he grabbed a knife off the counter and slit his wrist right in front of me. It was so awful.

Blood was everywhere. Scotty wrapped his wrist in a towel and took off on his motorcycle. I frantically tried to scrub all the blood out of the carpet in the bathroom so my step-father, who hadn't been awakened by all the noise, wouldn't see it. I felt really awful about how I had hurt Scotty.

After his attempted suicide, Scotty told Christine McVie, who was very much in love with Dennis, that I was sleep-ing with his father. I was about to start school then, in the seventh grade. Christine called me the night before my first day of class. "Sophie," she said, "I always welcomed you into my home. I did often wonder why Dennis took you shopping and why he paid so much attention to you, but I didn't have any idea what was really going on. When I was your age, I wasn't screwing my boyfriend's father. I was playing with dolls."

I felt really bad. It was hard for me to go to school the next day. There was no one there I could talk to. I couldn't relate to my classmates, whose lives were so different from mine. The only friends in whom I did confide were the older girls I met at the clubs I went to at night, girls who were not a part of my everyday life.

Dennis seemed oblivious to how his son and his girl-friend felt. He didn't stop seeing me. Sometimes he came over during the day and my mom would invite him in. He'd sit down at the piano in our music room and play. He even flirted with my mom one time. She was all giggly over him and it made me sick. I never told her what was going on, but it seemed to me that she must have known.

Dennis also continued his late-night visits, now on school nights. I'd go out with him, and we'd do drugs and maybe have sex. Then he'd drop me at home to sleep for a few hours. My stepfather would wake me early in the morning for school, never knowing that I had been awake and out partying most of the night.

I was trying to go to school during the day and function as a normal twelve-year-old girl, while at night I lived the life of a deranged thirty-year-old woman.

When I was really tired, I would call Dennis after my last class let out and ask him to pick me up. The black Corniche would pull up right in front of the school building and I'd get in. The other girls thought it was just too cool. I loved showing off the fact that I had the drummer from the Beach Boys picking me up from school.

One day when Dennis arrived at school he said, "Why don't you ask one of your girlfriends to come along?" I thought, "Why not?" and asked one of my friends to join us. We drove down to the marina and climbed aboard Dennis's boat. After a while he started to flirt with my friend, which made me really jealous and upset. I began to feel as though everything he had been saying to me was a big lie. I wasn't so special to him after all.

By this time not only Scotty and Christine McVie but also Scotty's mom, Carol, knew what was going on between Dennis and me. As I sat on the boat that day, fuming, the phone rang and I answered it. It was Carol. She had always liked me and took this opportunity to counsel me. "I want you to know that you're not the first young girl Dennis has been with, Sophie. You should not be around him. You'll wind up on drugs. He'll mess up your life. You should leave now and never see him again."

While Carol was telling me all this, I was watching Dennis hit on my girlfriend. I realized that I had made a very big mistake. I got into a screaming fight with Dennis, then grabbed my friend and left. We hitchhiked back to my house. I was in tears the whole time. My heart was broken at twelve by a man more than twice my age.

Dennis died years later. He drank too much one day and drowned while diving off his boat in Marina del Rey. Alcohol killed him, but he killed my innocence.

A Hitchhiker's Guide to L.A.

I met all sorts of people when hitchhiking around the city. I would always ask the men and women who picked me up if they got high. Most said yes. After all, it was the 1970s. People would often pull out a joint and offer it to me or drive to a liquor store and buy me liquor. Of course, I would always say I was much older than I was.

One time while hitchhiking I met a paraplegic guy. He had an ongoing prescription for Quaaludes because of his injury. I'd go over to his house and he would say, "If you show me your breasts, I'll give you a 'lude." I would lift up my shirt, quickly count to five, and then pull it down. He always wanted to up the ante. He'd want me to count to twenty for more pills, or he'd want to take Polaroids of my breasts for even more pills.

One day when I arrived at his house to "buy" some Quaaludes, he wasn't home. The door was open, so my girlfriend and I went into his house and took all of his drugs. We also took an expensive diamond ring. I was certainly being terrible, but so were a lot of the people I met.

Another guy I met while hitchhiking was an acting agent who had an office on Sunset Boulevard. He told me that he wanted to put me in commercials and invited me and my mother to his office. Because of my age, she had to sign a release before I could be photographed. So one day I convinced my mom to take me to his office. The building location and appearance seemed legitimate enough. While my mother sat in the reception area, its walls lined with pictures of beautiful women, this agent took me into his office for an "audition." As soon as we were behind closed doors he told me, "I have to see if you can act." He began to put his hands all over me, instructing me to pretend that I was in love with him. When I was hesitant, he assured me that all the other girls who became successful had to do the same thing. Then he went behind his desk and pulled down his pants. He told me to come over to him—he wanted a blow job.

I was horrified, but I thought this was what I had to do to make it. I walked over to him and got down on my knees behind his desk, but I couldn't go through with the act. I felt nauseated. I thought, "He's gross. God, my mother is sitting right there in the other room. This man has balls." I got up and left, and I never told my mom what happened. At the time I wished I could have done what he asked, because I really believed that it would help me get ahead. The agent later tried to arrange a photo session with me, but nothing ever came of it.

After that experience I learned to get out of similar tough spots by using my age. I'd say, "Do you know how young I am? Do you know how much trouble you could get in?" It gave me a lot of satisfaction to scare to death men like that sleazy agent.

I guess situations like this are why I never wanted to be an actress. Unlike so many other pretty girls in this town, I never had dreams of stardom. I knew too much early on about what was asked of girls who did, and I wasn't willing to play that game.

HOLLYWOOD AND SAN DIEGO, 1978

Meeting the Madam at Thirteen

When I was sleeping with Dennis Wilson, most of my older girlfriends were also having sex and doing drugs. It was a very fast crowd. One of the girls I knew suddenly started wearing really expensive clothes and jewelry and coming up with lots of money for drugs and fancy restaurants. When I found out that she was turning tricks for the money, she confided in me, "Sophie, I can introduce you to this woman I know named Cathy Black. I'm sure that you could do it, too, and make more money because of your age."

I was too young to understand what I was doing. I didn't really think of it as prostitution. It was more like an adventure, an exciting thing that the older girls were doing. Once again I just wanted to be in the fast crowd, like the cool older girls.

My friend did introduce me to Cathy Black, who with her husband, Al Black, ran a major call-girl ring. When Cathy found out that I was thirteen years old, it was love at first sight. To entice me to work for her, she glamorized the business. She said that the work was very professional and that most models and actresses as well as successful businesswomen did it to make money on the side. I was so naive then. I believed everything she said. Finally she threw in the clincher, "Why would you want to sleep with a boy your own age for nothing and get nothing out of it but a broken heart, when you could sleep with someone older and get paid for doing it?"

I understood exactly what she meant. After all, I had been sleeping with someone—Dennis Wilson—who left me with nothing but a broken heart. This way, I reasoned, I'd get something out of it. I loved clothes and I'd have money to get my pick of the latest fashions.

Cathy Black took me under her wing. She would pick me up at my house and personally take me to her clients. Brooke Shields had just been in the movie *Pretty Baby*, and I thought of myself as living the real-life version of the film. In my warped youthful perception, I thought that it was all so cool.

Cathy came by my house once when my mom was home. I told my mother that Cathy was taking me on a modeling interview. Cathy drove a Mercedes, wore Chanel from head to toe, and carried one of those little Chanel bags. She always looked very proper and together, like a successful businesswoman. My mom never checked up on Cathy or questioned anything.

Cathy *was* a successful businesswoman, of course—in the pimping business. She often took me to the Beverly Wilshire Hotel to meet clients. Once she brought me there to meet a guy who didn't want to have sex with me. He just wanted me to hang around. He taught me how to play chess, and we played together for a couple of hours. Most of the men, however, were not so easy to please. Many of her clients were Arabs—princes or royalty of some kind. Fortunately they usually weren't terribly unattractive, so it wasn't too bad at first.

I would take the money I earned, put it under my mattress, then spend most of it on clothes and makeup. I would loan my clothes to friends and let them use the expensive makeup I had purchased. I'd also give money to my friends. When we all went out on weekends, I'd make sure that everybody had a great time. Naturally my popularity rose.

One day Cathy Black asked me if I could get away from home for an entire night. That was no problem, I said to her. I would just tell my stepfather that I was spending the night with a friend. Cathy was thrilled. "You're going to hit the jackpot. You'll make big money on this trip."

A few days later Cathy and I flew down to San Diego. We arrived at an enormous estate, with waterfalls everywhere. It was like an Arabian palace. The huge mansion was filled with security guards and servants wearing white togas and carrying silver trays.

Cathy told me to go into the bathroom and change into an outfit that she had brought for me, presumably at the request of the man I was to meet. It was a little cheerleader's costume. I did as I was asked. When I came out of the bathroom, I noticed that there were now a lot of other girls in the house.

Cathy had always paid special attention to me and made me feel like I was her prized little girl, so I had no idea that there would be other girls there. They were older than me, and were all wearing long black trench coats. I wondered why I was in a cheerleader's outfit and they were all in trench coats. Cathy said that I didn't have to wear a trench coat because I was special and didn't have to do what they were doing.

Cathy had all of the girls in trench coats line up as music began to play. It was a strange, whining sort of Arabian music that irritated me. The girls started to take off their trench coats, revealing skimpy, sexy lingerie underneath. Then, suddenly, it was orgy time. Dozens of Arab men walked over to the girls, and everybody started having sex with everybody else. Sex acts were going on everywhere—on the chairs, on the floor, against the walls.

Cathy told me not to worry. I didn't have to be a part of the orgy. I was reserved for something special. She walked me down a long hallway to a bedroom where a man who must have been the real prince, or maybe just the richest one, was waiting for me. Very tall, skinny, and gawky-looking, he was probably the least attractive man I had ever seen. After Cathy left the room, he wanted to have sex with me. But he wanted anal sex, something I had never done before. I was really scared and began to cry, then I ran out of the room to find Cathy.

"He wants to have sex with me in my behind," I said to Cathy when I found her. "Well, go and do it then," she coaxed me. That wasn't at all what I had hoped to hear. I desperately wanted her to go back into the room and tell that ugly man how disgusting he was and to yell at him for trying to do such a thing to her special little girl. Then I wanted her to take me home. Instead Cathy pleaded with me, "Sophie, you'll get a lot more money. Just go on and do it."

I went back into that room and tried my best to accommodate him, but it hurt. The more he persisted, the harder I cried. Finally I told him that I just couldn't go through with it. I ran out of there crying, and when I found Cathy again, I admitted that I hadn't done as the man wanted. She said it was okay, but I felt really bad. I knew I had disappointed her. Cathy was like a mother to me. Since my own mother wasn't around much, Cathy was the only woman I confided in. I looked up to her, and I needed her approval.

After this experience with the Arab who wanted the back-door action, however, I started to make excuses when Cathy called and wanted me to see her clients. I was too afraid to do it anymore.

Scott Baio Couldn't Take What He Dished Out

I did have one sexual experience as a girl of thirteen that was innocent and nice, the way teenage romance is supposed to be. It was a brief affair with Scott Baio. He was only a couple of years older than me, and we simply liked each other. It didn't last, however.

We had just begun seeing each other when Scott, who was recovering from a recent bout of tonsillitis, began taking medication that made his face break out. One night after one of our dates, he dropped me off at my house. As I opened the car door to get out, he joked about my breasts, saying something like, "See ya, Tits." He had said that to me before, but I never did like it, so I retorted, "Yeah, okay, see ya, Zits." Scott never called me again after that. This teenage star could dish it out, but he couldn't take it.

Roger Daltrey Is Too Married for Me

*W*hen I was also about fourteen I had a friend who loved the rock group the Who and the band's lead singer, Roger Daltrey. They were in town for a concert and I promised my friend that I would figure out where the band was staying and get us in to meet Roger. I was good at finding out where the "in crowd" things were happening.

I found out that Roger and the band were staying at L'Hermitage Hotel in Beverly Hills. My girlfriend and I showed up at the hotel the next day, hoping to meet Roger. The road manager immediately spotted us walking through the lobby and suggested that we hang out by the pool. As we were sitting on pool chairs, sunning ourselves, a different guy appeared out of nowhere and said to me, "Mr. Daltrey would like to see you in his room." I felt kind of bad because it was my girlfriend, not me, who had the thing for Roger Daltrey. I promised her that I would go and see what he wanted.

When I arrived at his room, Roger opened the door wearing a robe. He had obviously just gotten out of the shower. I thought he was definitely a handsome guy, but it bothered me that he was married. He lay down on the king-size bed and said, "Come on, honey. Come over here with me." He didn't even ask me my name. I didn't move but looked at him and blurted out, "What about your wife?" He gave me the most exasperated look, and I'm sure he was thinking, "You little bitch, who do you think you are?"

I tried to make it better. "I'm sorry, Mr. Daltrey. It's not me who likes you. It's my girlfriend. I'll tell her to come up here."

He seemed kind of embarrassed and told me to just go. Before we left the hotel, though, the road manager gave us tickets to that night's concert. At the show we were almost trampled by the crowd rushing up to the stage, and we were taken backstage for safety. Then my girlfriend and I were invited to party at the hotel after the show with the rest of the band, including Pete Townshend. Of course we went. Roger Daltrey, however, wasn't there. My friend was disappointed, but I hoped he was seeing his wife.

HOLLYWOOD, 1978

Call of the Wild

During spring-break party weekend for college kids in Palm Springs (I was only in eighth grade but never missed a party) I started dating a nice guy who was going to UCLA. He was Jewish and smart and his father was president of a big television production company. He was a good influence on me, and I cleaned up my act for a while. I did better in school. I quit sneaking out and quit lying to my parents, and I even began to get close to my boyfriend's family.

Unfortunately one of my older girlfriends reentered my life. One night she took me to El Privado, a private club on the Sunset Strip above the old Carlos 'n Charlie's restaurant. My friend was then seeing Rick James, a big Motown artist who had a number-one hit song at that time. The club was owned by Shep Gordon, a music manager who handled singers like Peter Frampton. Shep was at the door when we arrived. He knew that I was underage, but he didn't care. He told me that as long as I stayed cool, didn't tell anyone my age, and didn't drink, I could come on in and have fun.

Later that night I left the club with my friend and Rick James and went to a hotel room where they were staying. We sat around together, and they freebased cocaine. It was the first time I'd ever seen anyone do that, but they didn't let me try it. After they went off into the bedroom, I left for home. Later I found out that Rick had gone into convulsions in a seizure from the drugs. My girlfriend told me she freaked out and ran naked down the hotel hallway screaming for help. An ambulance finally arrived and took him to the hospital.

116

You might expect that hearing about this experience sent me running back to my nice boyfriend from UCLA. It didn't. The clubs, the parties, and the hip people were all more attractive to me than what he offered. I started going to Shep's club more and more. When my boyfriend's final exams were over, I broke up with him. At the tender age of fourteen I had decided that I wanted to lead a very rough life. And during the next five years, it only got rougher.

HOLLYWOOD HILLS, 1979

Breakdowns and Broken Homes

Around this time my mother and my stepfather split up. My mom had been having an affair, or maybe more than one, and my stepdad learned the truth. He was a really good man and he loved her, but he couldn't take it anymore. He wanted a divorce.

My mother suffered a nervous breakdown and locked herself in her room for what seemed like a year. At the same time my older stepsister also had a breakdown. Once I had to stop her from drinking a glass of insecticide. Another time she was standing in the middle of Mulholland, naked, and the fire department had to bring her home. Yet another time she tried to light herself on fire.

Somehow my younger brother managed to stay sane during all of this. He just kept his focus on school and blocked all the craziness out. He was the good one, and I was still the wild one.

The day the moving van arrived I had nowhere to go. My mother was moving to a one-room guest house. My brother was going to live with my stepfather, who by now was getting remarried. But I didn't know where I was going. It was the worst feeling in the world. I wasn't really welcome at my stepfather's new house because I was such a troublemaker. He had really had it with me. He and his new wife agreed that I could stay there for a while until I figured out what I was going to do, but I didn't even have a room there and was sleeping on the couch.

At Carlos 'n Charlie's, I met a girl, Darlene, and we became fast friends. She was much older than me and very tall and beautiful, with jet-black hair and cat-green eyes. Darlene lived in a guest house off Woodrow Wilson Drive in the Hollywood Hills. I moved out of my stepfather's new house and in with Darlene. Then I dropped out of school, having just completed the eighth grade. My life became drugs, parties, men, and more drugs.

My stepfather would occasionally bring me money, but reluctantly. He didn't know whether I was going to use the money to buy drugs or to buy food. I hardly ever saw my mother. She was still zigzagging in and out of reality.

I liked Darlene, but living with her was chaotic and awful. The family living in the main house had a little kid whose mother was a major drug addict. She was always falling down and hurting herself and the kid was always crying. The final straw for me came when a couple of this woman's drugged-out friends broke into the guest house where Darlene and I lived and stole all my clothes. I soon found another place to live.

HOTEL CALIFORNIA, 1980

Girls for My Landlord

I met a man, John, a major player in real estate at the time, who lived in a great big pink house off Miller Drive in the Hollywood Hills. People used to call the house "Hotel California." It was part of the old Errol Flynn estate and John was happy to carry on the randy traditions of the old swashbuckler Flynn. He would sit in his office in front of a humongous desk and young girls would parade through all the time. He dated Victoria Principal at one time, and was very fond of Hugh Hefner's Playboy Playmates. A lot of the *Playboy* magazine centerfolds were photographed up at the pink house.

John liked me and I liked his cocaine. One night when we were doing some coke together, I spoke to him about my unhappy living situation at Darlene's place. He said that I could move in with him. In exchange for my room and board, I took care of the house. That included doing the grocery shopping, the cleaning, and supervising the pool man and gardener.

John was very scary-looking and I didn't want to have sex with him. By then I had learned how to maneuver my way out of sleeping with anybody I didn't want to. I knew John wouldn't bother me if there were plenty of other pretty girls around the house. I invited lots of girls I knew over to keep old John happy. Once the party was in full swing, I was able to go to my room and get some sleep.

I was fifteen years old at the time and was hanging around people like Shannon Tweed and other Playboy Playmates. They would come over to John's house to exercise and take aerobics classes on the big dance floor in the house, which had a wall of mirrors and ballet bars. I'd hang out with them and they'd tell me how cool and cute I was. I just bought it all.

Naturally, with all the access to drugs at John's house, I started doing more and more cocaine.

THE FORUM, LOS ANGELES AND
PALM SPRINGS, 1981

The King of the Court

While living at John's I went to a few Los Angeles Lakers games with an older girlfriend. It was inevitable, I suppose, that I would meet the infamous Lakers owner, Jerry Buss. Jerry, who was known to like young girls, invited me to sit in his box one night. The next day he sent flowers and a gold Longines watch. At sixteen I thought Longines watches were just so cool.

Jerry started giving me and my friends tickets to the games. Then he invited me up to his estate, Pickfair, to have lunch with him. Not long afterward he invited me to go to Palm Springs. I flew there from L.A., and we stayed at a hotel he owned, the Ocotillo Lodge, which was a real popular place. I had my own room at the hotel, and Jerry didn't bother me, but John Rockwell, a sidekick of Jerry's, got drunk, broke into my room, and attacked me. I pushed a TV set at him and it hit his mouth, causing his lip to bleed all over the place. Jerry later found out what happened and apparently thought it was funny.

When the weekend was over, Jerry and I took his limo back to L.A. We were sitting in the backseat, and suddenly his hands were all over me. I thought he was disgusting.

He smelled bad and looked worse. He used to brush his hair in a circle on his head and put hair spray on it. I felt that I couldn't be with him for all the money in the world.

Unfortunately that tune changed—and it didn't take all the money in the world, either. When we got back to L.A., Jerry kept calling me. I had heard from other girls that it was a cool thing to be with Jerry Buss, that Jerry set up his women in apartments, with clothes, sometimes a car. I wanted that, too. I decided that having sex with Jerry was something that I had to do. So I went up to his house one night. When I arrived he was in the shower, wearing a polka-dot shower cap. Everything about him just repulsed me beyond belief. I lay on the bed and closed my eyes, pretending that he was someone else, trying to block out what was happening. But it did happen, and I was the one who let it happen. After that I just wanted to get high.

LAKE TAHOE, 1980

A Welcome from Mr. Kotter

*J*erry Buss was a big poker player. He would have endless poker games going on in his kitchen, and I met a number of guys who were regulars at the game. One guy I met was Gabe Kaplan, the star of the TV series *Welcome Back, Kotter*. Gabe and I exchanged phone numbers and he called soon after and invited me to go with him to Lake Tahoe.

Naturally I went. I wanted to go to Tahoe for the fun and the gambling and I figured that a rendezvous with Gabe was the price. Mr. Kotter turned out to be just a real straight guy. There were no drugs with him, and I don't know if he even knew my age. Unfortunately I wasn't much into Gabe—to me he was yesterday's news. Also he looked like my real dad and that was a little eerie and strange.

Hitting Hefner's Blacklist

When I was spending time with Jerry Buss I also met a man named Steve Powers, who was a sidekick of Hugh Hefner's. A lot of guys like Jerry Buss and Hugh Hefner had men working for them who were nothing more than personal pimps. They drove expensive cars and wore beautiful clothes, but they had no function other than pleasing their master. And that usually meant finding him pretty girls.

Steve Powers wanted to take me and a few other girls up to Hefner's house for dinner and a movie screening, an event Hefner hosted every Sunday night. I never turned down a good time.

We arrived to find a fabulous feast of lobster, prime rib, and rich, hearty American food. Then we saw a movie, but I left before it was over. I wanted to look around the mansion. I wandered into the Jacuzzi room, known as "the cave." I knew everyone would be heading there once the movie was over. I noticed this very weird thing—a specially designed sex chair—in the middle of the Jacuzzi room. I had heard about it. The whole idea freaked me out. I decided to leave before things got too strange, and I went back into the house to see about getting a ride. I saw Hugh Hefner and asked him if there was a car on the property that could take me home. He looked at me and asked how old I was. I told him fifteen. His face got pale, and he said, "Oh, thank you very much. Yes, I have a car that will take you right home. Come back when you're eighteen."

I was supposedly put on Hefner's blacklist and not allowed back in until I was eighteen. But I did manage to sneak into parties at the Playboy Mansion a few times. I just changed my name and in I went.

NEW YORK, 1981

Good-bye L.A., Hello New York

From time to time I got in touch with my mother— usually when I needed something. She had begun to get herself together again. After the divorce was finalized, she moved to an apartment in Venice. When I turned sixteen she bought me a new car, a BMW, from part of her settlement.

At that old age of sixteen I felt like I knew the whole scene in Los Angeles and decided that I wanted to go to New York. I told my mom, "I need three hundred dollars really bad. I want to go to New York, get my life together, and start modeling." She believed me and gave me the money.

I didn't know anyone in New York except a guy who lived out on Long Island. It was cold and snowy at his place and I was miserable. I called a friend back in L.A. and asked if she knew anyone in the city whom I could call. She gave me the number of a guy named Doug, who she said would show me a really good time. Doug turned out to be a big gambler. When I called him he was in Atlantic City so he sent a car to pick me up in New York and take me there to meet him.

He seemed stunned when he saw me. "How old are you?" he immediately asked. I told him the truth and he seemed to feel bad for me. To him I was obviously a lost kid in the big city. He told me that he would take me back to Manhattan, and I could stay at his apartment until I found a job and got my life together. He could tell that I had been through a lot.

While staying with Doug I didn't find a job, but it didn't take long for me to find my way into the New York club scene. I hung out at places like Studio 54, did drugs, and met people from the music and film industries.

One night I met a girl, Susan, who became my new best friend. She was the most beautiful girl I had ever seen, and she took me to meet all sorts of people—people who would share their drugs with me.

One night Susan took me to an expensive restaurant and, as we were enjoying our meal, a diner from across the room had a bottle of wine sent over to our table. Our admirer was Adnan Khashoggi, one of the richest men in New York. He invited us to join him later that night at a party at the Olympic Towers. We went. All kinds of gorgeous women were there. A man who worked for Khashoggi, Victor, another right-hand-man pimp type, asked me if I'd like to go to Paris. Soon it was good-bye New York, hello Paris.

PARIS, 1981

Life With Khashoggi

I arrived in Paris and checked into the big lavender Hôtel Nouveau Park Élysée, courtesy of Adnan Khashoggi. Adnan never pressured me and was sweet and caring, so I didn't mind sleeping with him. But I didn't see him very much and was alone and bored much of the time. I called friends in New York and asked them if they knew anyone in Paris I could call. A friend told me to call a guy named Patrick. I connected with him, and he took me out to a nightclub, the Apocalypse.

At that club I met Anthony Delon, the son of actor Alain Delon. I fell head over heels for Anthony. It had been quite a while since I had been with somebody my own age, and we really had fun together. He took me all around Paris on the back of his motorcycle. I was in love with love, with Anthony, and with Paris.

The trip ended too soon, and I had to return to the States. Not long afterward, however, Adnan invited me back to Paris. This time I recruited a bunch of my girl-friends for the trip—and for Adnan. We took a private jet and first stopped in Spain at Marbella, where Adnan had a villa on the Costa del Sol. At the villa there was one closet filled with Dior gowns and another filled with mink coats. They were secured with chains, like the ones used in department stores to prevent theft. Adnan would frequently fly groups of girls to his villa, and the girls he liked would go home with a mink coat or a Dior gown in addition to a handful of cash. I think that a girl had to be really good to get the mink coat and the gown. None of my girlfriends from that trip went home with a mink. At dinner one evening, however, we sat down to a gorgeous table set with the finest crystal and china, as well as a little something extra—different pieces of jewelry on all of our plates.

By this time Adnan and I had become pretty good friends. I reminded him of another L.A. woman who used to supply him with girls. She's now very prominent in show business and happily married. People used to call me the junior version of her, because we were both in the Khashoggi circle, getting girls for him. Adnan was with all the girls I brought to him, and he seemed to have a pretty good time. While my girls were taking care of Adnan, I ran off and had sex on the beach with his young gorgeous masseur. As much as I liked Adnan, the affair with his masseur was a bit more interesting.

After a week or so in Spain, we all flew to Paris. When we got there I tried to find Anthony Delon again. By now, however, he was with Princess Stephanie, so our short romance was over. I was depressed about it and started doing more and more drugs. Patrick, the friend who had first taken me to the club where I met Anthony, introduced me to heroin. In the beginning I just snorted the drug. The other girls on the trip were into drugs, too, but not heroin. Despite the money, clothes, and jewelry that had been showered on me, I was sinking very fast into a major drug addiction. I was a very unhappy young girl. I didn't have a mom or dad I felt I could turn to. I turned, instead, to heroin.

NEW YORK, 1982

Big Problems in the Big Apple

Despite my ambitions I was never really much of a madam, for Adnan or anyone. Perhaps it was because

I was usually the youngest. The girls would start to negotiate with me, and I just couldn't handle it. Adnan was stood up by girls more than once when I was in charge. Also I think I was so lousy at it because I felt guilty, like I was sacrificing them for my own benefit. As much as I tried, I knew it was wrong.

I went back to New York and met Johnny Rock, a guy who owned a nightclub and was well connected in the music business. I was crazy about him, and it wasn't long before I moved in with him.

When Adnan came back to New York, he called me, and I went to see him. He gave me an incredible necklace from Van Cleef & Arpels. He wanted to continue seeing me. It was hard to turn down the gifts Adnan showered on me, even though I loved Johnny. I thought I could handle seeing both Adnan and Johnny at the same time.

One night I came back to Johnny's place late at night after being with Adnan. I showed Johnny a piece of jewelry Adnan had given me. He was amazed. He had never seen anything like it before. I told him about my trips to Europe with Adnan on the private jet and about my girlfriends' $10,000 fees and shopping trips. It didn't seem to bother him. He had no idea, however, how much it was tearing me up inside.

Sometime later, Lou Adler, who was a friend of Johnny's, called to say that his stepdaughter was having some problems and that she wanted to come to New York to pursue an acting and modeling career. She was Victoria Sellers, Peter Sellers's daughter. A really skinny kid who seemed nice, innocent, and rather naive, Victoria moved in with Johnny and me. She used to love to look at the clothes in my closet. I had a lot of dresses by Alaïa from my trips to Paris. Victoria would say, ''You have so many Alaïa dresses.

I just can't believe how many you have. Can I borrow one?"

"Sure, help yourself, borrow anything you like." I had no concept of the value of anything I had. It didn't matter. It had all come so easily—or so it seemed. One day Victoria was trying on one of my Alaïa dresses worth about $2,000. She was smoking and dropped her cigarette on it, leaving a burn in the front. But I didn't care. I didn't value anything. Mostly I didn't value myself.

NEW YORK CITY, 1982

Drugs and Suicide Go Together

I was now seventeen and my drug habit was growing much faster than I was. I had figured out a way to get into Johnny's safe, where he kept his drugs, and I started doing more and more of everything. I was pathetic. One night—I don't really know exactly what triggered it—I was so unhappy that I didn't want to live anymore. I slit my wrist, just like Scotty Wilson had done in my house years earlier.

That night Johnny had people over at the apartment. They were in the living room while I was in the bedroom attempting to kill myself. Clive Davis, president of Arista Records, and singer John Waite were there. Johnny came into the bedroom and found me sprawled out on the floor, with blood everywhere. He screamed, "What the hell happened? What are you doing?" He yelled for help and everyone came running into the bedroom. Clive Davis helped Johnny get me up and wrap a towel around my wrist.

Davis looked at Johnny and said, "I can't even get a girl to shave her legs for me, let alone slit her wrist."

Johnny rushed me to Bellevue Hospital in a cab. I was afraid that they would put me in a crazy ward, so I kept saying that it had been a shaving accident—the razor had slipped.

My explanation didn't seem to have very much credibility. Everyone looked at me like I was insane. The doctor grilled me, demanding to know what I had taken. Johnny yelled at me right along with the doctor. "Tell him what you took. Tell him everything," he pleaded.

"I took a Quaalude," I said.

"What else?" the doctor pressed me.

"I took a Placidyl," I added.

"What else did you take?" he demanded.

"I had some coke."

"Is that all?"

"I did some heroin," I finally said. "That's all."

Dumbfounded, Johnny looked at me and said, "Heroin? You did heroin?" He was so furious that he just walked out and left me there. The doctors kept me in the hospital overnight. The next day Johnny came and took me back to his apartment, but told me to straighten up my act or get lost. I didn't want to leave so I tried to cool it a bit. I wasn't very successful.

NEW YORK CITY, 1982

Midnight Therapy on Fifth Avenue

During this time I knew a guy named Marco who lived in a beautiful penthouse on Fifth Avenue. He owned lots of nightclubs. Every night, after the action at the clubs wound down, everyone would sit around a really large glass table in his living room. People like Adnan's daughter, various Kennedys, and tennis player Vitas Gerulaitis all loved going to Marco's.

He would conduct these group therapy-type sessions around his glass table. He would pass coke around and when it was your turn to talk you got to take a hit of the cocaine. You had to talk about yourself and what you wanted to do with your life. Then Marco would grill you. "Enough of that," he'd say. "Cut the bullshit. Get to the truth. What do you really want?"

Everyone was nervous when their turn came, but they all wanted that coke in front of them. That was the real "truth." Those nights were some of the most fun evenings I've ever had, because people were communicating and revealing their innermost thoughts. It was more intimacy than I was used to having, and it was always a well-picked group. Marco was always good at putting people together.

One night one of Marco's regulars, Vitas Gerulaitis, was busted for coke. Things got scary after that. People thought that phones were being tapped. Tony Goebbel, Vitas's best friend, was going to take the rap for Vitas. I spent the night with Tony in Marco's apartment before he went to jail. It was a pretty sad night—the end of the fun at Marco's. I felt like the party was coming to an end.

ST. MORITZ, SWITZERLAND, 1982

Prince Charming Is a Fantasy

After the Vitas bust I went back to L.A. for a while, where I met a guy, Jamie, who wanted me and a bunch of my girlfriends to fly to St. Moritz, Switzerland, to spend time with an Arab prince. I agreed and rounded up some girlfriends. We arrived at The Badrutt's Palace Hotel in the Alps, which is one of the most beautiful places on earth. It was the most amazing hotel I'd ever seen and in my short life I'd seen a few. The pool had a huge glass dome over the top of it. Snow covered the glass, which made it seem like a magical Christmas card come to life. There were also horse-drawn carriages that transported the guests from the hotel door to the ski slopes. It was the first time I'd ever skied, and I just loved the whole experience.

Everything we wanted was on the house, courtesy of the prince. My girlfriends and I bought clothes and bathing suits at the hotel shop for use in the spa and indoor pool. I took a swim the first day and went for a massage. The prince also happened to be getting a massage at the same time. He told me later on that he saw me and didn't know that I was there to meet him. When he figured it out, he was very happy.

We had a fine time together. The only trouble was that I found myself liking this prince a lot. One night we were out having a romantic dinner, and I was cold so he gave me his jacket. While still wearing it, I went into the ladies' room and noticed a slip of paper in one of the pockets. Another girl who was on the trip, a pretty blonde who was older than me, had written him a note after their night together. It read, "It was really nice being with you last night. Come

131

to my room anytime. My door is always open to you." I had been with him that same night, too, so I felt pretty stupid about my feelings for him. I crumpled up the note and tossed it away. Seeing the note, however, was a jolt of reality, reminding me why Jamie had invited me in the first place. In situations like that it was always hard for me not to hope that something special would happen. In the end, of course, nothing special happened between me and Prince Charming in the romantic hotel.

NEW YORK CITY, 1982

Back to the Emergency Room

After the trip to St. Moritz, I flew to New York. Boxer Gerry Cooney was in the city for a big match and was staying at the Waldorf-Astoria on Park Avenue. I ran into Tony Goebbel, who had done his time for the Vitas drug episode, and he invited me to go to Cooney's suite at the Waldorf for a little pre-fight celebration.

The first thing I saw when we arrived at the Cooney suite was a naked belly dancer doing flips. All kinds of people were there, and all of them, including Cooney, were doing lots of coke. I wondered how this guy was going to survive in the ring tomorrow when he was coked out of his mind tonight.

As it turned out, he wasn't the only one coked out of his or her mind. I woke up the next morning in an unfamiliar hospital emergency room somewhere in Harlem. Tony later told me that I had overdosed and passed out. Because Cooney's fight was the next day, everyone had panicked.

They rolled me up in a Persian rug from the floor of the hotel suite and had security sneak me out the back door. I was dumped off at a hospital in Harlem to avoid any publicity that might hurt Cooney and the fight.

I woke up in the emergency room just as they were about to pump my stomach. A cap was on my head, and they were prepping me to put a tube down my throat. I pleaded with them to stop, telling them that I was okay and didn't need my stomach pumped. They acquiesced and moved me from the emergency room to another room that had baths for people with lice. The whole experience was just awful.

Doug, my first friend in New York, came to my rescue again. I lived at his place for a while after the hospital ordeal. Many people I knew were now afraid to be around me. I was still underage, and nobody wanted to take the rap if I ended up dead from my heavy drug use.

Johnny Rock was still in and out of my life and he offered to send me to a ranch in New Mexico owned by an art dealer friend of his named Danny. He thought I would be able to clean up and dry out at this guy's place. I said okay and soon left town.

LOS ANGELES, 1983

Speedballs on the Way to Santa Fe

I detoured to L.A. before going to Danny's Santa Fe ranch. Johnny and I had a big fight because he had other girls coming to his house. Upset with him and lonely because he was sending me away by myself, I decided to go score some drugs to take on the trip. The dealer I went to was shooting up speedballs, which are heroin and coke mixed together. I decided to try one. I lay down on the floor, stuck out my arm, and said, "Just do it, stick it in, I'm ready."

I had always been frightened of needles, so I covered my eyes with my free arm. When the dealer stuck the needle in my vein, a warm feeling came over my body, and there was a buzzing sound in my ears. It was like no other feeling I had ever felt in my life. It was better than freebasing, better than snorting anything. It was an unbelievable feeling of warmth engulfing my entire being. I just checked out completely and was floating somewhere. I was supposed to be on my way to New Mexico to dry out, clean up, and recover, but from that point on all I wanted to do was shoot heroin and coke.

SANTA FE, 1983

Near Death in the Desert

Danny owned a big ranch out in the middle of nowhere near Santa Fe—and he kept plenty of coke at the house. Before I arrived, Johnny had probably told Danny not to give me any drugs, but why Johnny thought I would dry out around a guy who did coke, I don't know. Yet here I was. I didn't have any heroin left, so I went into his bathroom one night and shot up cocaine. It's very bad to shoot coke if you have nothing to come down on. It's probably the worst thing that you can do to yourself.

I went into convulsions and fell through the bathroom

door. Danny stood there over me. He saw the needle in my arm and thought I was going to die right there on the spot. He went into a panic, pleading with me not to die. When I came to, he looked at me and said, "Thank God you're alive." What he meant, of course, was thank God I didn't die in his house. He told me that he'd thought he was going to have to take me out into the desert and bury me somewhere rather than explain the whole thing to the cops. That was it for the Santa Fe rehab and recovery. I was back on the next plane to L.A.

LOS ANGELES, 1984

Jack Nicholson and the Junkie

After I got back to L.A., it wasn't long before I turned into a complete junkie. Danny had given me a painting to deliver to Jack Nicholson, which I did as soon as I got to town. Jack was really nice to me when we met and afterward called to ask me to come over and hang out. I didn't call him back for a while. I was too busy trying to get money for drugs and shooting up. One day I called him, hoping I could get some money or drugs from him, and he invited me up to his house.

Even though I had track marks all over my arms, Jack still wanted to have sex with me. All he could talk about, however, was Anjelica Huston, who was his girlfriend at the time.

He took me into a bedroom that looked awfully small. I realized it was his guest room, which I thought was strange. If you like a girl you don't take her into the guest room—you go into your own bedroom. But I guess that was reserved for Anjelica. We fooled around, and to me it was no big deal. It must have been good enough for Jack, I guess, because he called me several times after that. But I was more into getting high than being with anybody. I just wanted to be alone with my dope and my syringe.

LOS ANGELES, 1984

Hitting a Horrible Bottom

I became close friends during that time with Jason Bronson, Charles Bronson's son. We would run around L.A. and score drugs together. His father would find out where each drug dealer his son bought from lived and would pound on the dealer's window, threatening to have the dealer busted and sent to jail if he ever sold drugs to his son again.

Charles put Jason into rehab, but it just didn't work. Jason eventually died from drugs.

Also, my beautiful friend Darlene, with whom I lived when my mother and stepfather first divorced and who had a bad drug habit, died. To this day no one knows if she was killed by her drug-dealer boyfriend or if she committed suicide. She left a small son behind. Dick Engle, another friend of mine from New York, also overdosed and died. A Russian friend from New York was shot and killed over drugs. People were dying all around me because of drugs, but it wasn't enough to get me to stop. I lived to get high.

I was now a full-blown heroin addict walking Sunset Boulevard, looking for tricks to pay for my highs. I would do anything for drugs. I went from traveling with Adnan Khashoggi and being one of the most popular girls on the whole New York-L.A.-Paris circuit to being a streetwalker on the Strip—all so I could get money for heroin.

At one point I was hanging out with a really scary Persian guy who was an addict and a drug dealer. We were staying at the Holiday Inn on Sunset. He fell asleep before I did, and while he was sleeping I used all of his drugs. When he woke up and saw that everything was gone, he grabbed me, held my head, and started bashing me in the face with his knee. I heard this awful sound. It felt like my whole cheekbone was crushed.

I ran out of the hotel, a complete mess. My face was swelling. I was completely dazed. People on the street were staring at me. Somebody finally stopped their car and took me to the hospital. In the emergency room they took X rays and discovered that my face was fractured. There was nothing that could be done, however, except put ice packs on it and let it heal. I looked really horrible, like the Elephant Man.

Previous to this I had been in the same hospital for abscesses on my arms. Since I shot up so much, I had no veins left and would get these abscesses from missing the veins. A young doctor took care of me then and tried to help me. He gave me phone numbers for rehab centers and even gave me his pager number. I could tell by how he looked at me at the time that he thought I was going to die very soon.

This nice doctor was also at the hospital the night I was brought in after having been beaten up. By the way he looked at me when he saw me, I just knew that this was the end. I knew I was destroying myself. I was incredibly skinny. I couldn't wear short sleeves because I had scars all over my arms. Now my face was battered and disfigured.

After I left the hospital I went to my mom's house. She

now had a one-bedroom apartment in Beverly Hills and I had been staying with her when I wasn't on the floor of a shooting gallery somewhere.

My mom screamed when she saw me. I looked so awful that I frightened her, and at first she wouldn't let me in. Finally she did and called the police. The police asked me who did this to me, but I wouldn't tell them. I was too scared.

I didn't stop using drugs then, but I was at a definite turning point. During this time a friend from grade school had reentered my life and was trying to help me. She was really religious and kept asking me to go to church with her. She would lecture me and talk about God. I didn't want to think about any of that, I guess because it gives you a conscience and makes you start to feel guilty.

My friend also researched all the rehab places in town. None of them wanted to take me because I didn't have insurance or any money. She finally got in touch with a county facility, a methadone clinic, and begged them to take me. She told them that she knew I was going to die. Somehow she got them to agree to admit me.

By this time, between my experience in the hospital, a few trips to church, and lectures from my friend, I decided to try to change things. I agreed to go to rehab, and my brother drove me to the methadone clinic. I smoked heroin on tinfoil in his car the whole way to the place, telling him, "This is my last high."

I was in rehab for a total of nine months. After you dry out in the medical clinic, they put you in a place that has an open-door policy. You are supposed to stay there, but you aren't locked in. One time, after I had been sober three months, I snuck out. Naturally I hitchhiked, and as soon as a guy picked me up I asked him if he got high. He said yeah, so I asked him to take me to my old drug dealer's house.

He said he would, but he drove past the place. I got really frightened. He took us to a residential area, ordered me to get into the backseat, and raped me. I was terrified. When you're not on drugs you're so emotional. You feel everything—the fear, horror, and disgust.

He let me out of the car and drove off. I knocked on the door of a nearby house and told the people who answered that I had just been raped. They let me call the police, who came and drove me back to the rehab place. I felt so stupid. What had happened to me was a huge dose of reality. I was hit with my choices—I could either stay in this place and get myself together or go back out there to my old life and get raped or killed. The next day I had to stand in front of the whole facility and ask to be accepted back. They let me back in, and I didn't leave again until I completed the program six months later.

BEVERLY HILLS, 1996

A Happy Ending

I was a very young teenager hooked on cocaine and then heroin. I slept with rich and famous men who were two, three, four, and even five times my age. I had sex for money and pimped my friends for drugs, for clothes, and to travel the world. I did it to be cool. But by the time I was eighteen, there was no pleasure left.

I was lucky. When I found my way into the drug rehab twelve years ago, I made a decision to turn my life around. Choosing to take my life back, deciding to change, was the really hard part.

In addition to stopping the drugs, I also needed to change my need for the money, the clothes, and the rich friends. I needed to free myself of the world I lived in that made drugs seem so necessary. I wanted another chance. I desperately wanted to start over and have a new life.

When I got out of rehab I moved into the guest room at my girlfriend's house. I found a job working in a clothing store and day by day, inch by inch, I began to transform my life.

From the day I got out of the L.A. rehab onward, I have never gotten high. I no longer have to fight the urge to fall back into that life. The women friends I have now support themselves by legitimate work. They are not party girls, nor are they trying to be glamorous beauty queens looking for a rich guy. I learned, and so have my friends, when to say no. It's true that a lot of men don't like women who say what they want and who won't be pushed around. If a woman asserts herself, she might not have dates every night. But when a guy does come along, he's a better guy . . . and it's real.

I'm married now and have two wonderful, incredible kids. As I think about my past and the two beautiful children that I am blessed with today, I am so thankful that I was able to change. Every moment I am grateful for my healthy children. I will do everything I can to make sure they never have to experience anything like what I went through.

I wanted to tell my story because it's different. It's rare that someone survives what I went through as a child and is able to live a normal, stable, and sober life. From time to time I see some of the women I knew back in the days when I was involved with drugs and partying. Many of them haven't changed. They're just older, not wiser. I hope and pray that they will one day change their lives, too. They're still so caught up in the easy money and the drugs. I would guess that only one in a hundred girls, or maybe even fewer, leave a life of drugs and prostitution and go on to find a normal and happy life. I know that I am very fortunate to be that one in a hundred or more. And I'm happy that I lived to tell the tale.

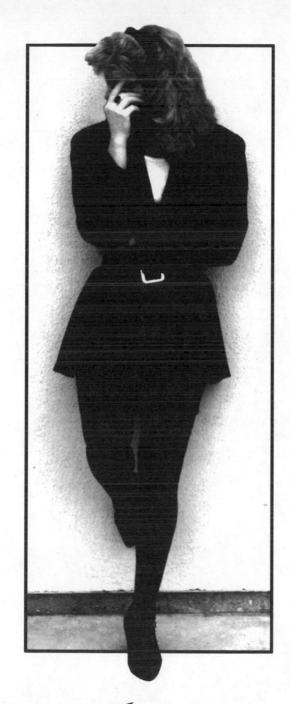

Jewel

HEIGHT:	*5'5"*
HAIR:	*Honey brown*
EYES:	*Hazel*
WEIGHT:	*105*
PROFESSION:	*Unemployed*
BORN:	*Los Angeles, California*
HOBBIES:	*Roller blading, going to museums, travelling, and scuba diving*
EDUCATION:	*Eastern prep schools; B.A. from Harvard University*
FIRST SEXUAL EXPERIENCE:	*At age seventeen, with boyfriend at boarding school*
GOALS & DESIRES:	*To reunite with my family and to find legitimate employment*
SEXUAL FANTASY:	*To have a man love me for who I am*
DRUGS:	*Cocaine, Nyquil mixed with Valium, Ecstasy*
HAPPIEST MEMORY:	*My senior year at high school*
WORST EXPERIENCE:	*Returning to Los Angeles as an adult*
SEX PARTNERS:	*Bjorn Borg, Paramount Pictures executive, porn stars, Hollywood film agents, and more*

BEVERLY HILLS

An Inauspicious Beginning

When I was born, in February 1968, my parents lived in Beverly Hills near the Cielo Drive house where, in August of 1969, Sharon Tate and four others were murdered by Charles Manson and his followers. I was only a year and a half when the horrendous slayings took place, and my family moved from the area shortly thereafter. Perhaps that early event was a bad omen for my future. Perhaps it is why I've felt cursed so much of my life, why it seems that—despite the privileges and opportunities I've had, including my Harvard education—the bad luck in my life has outweighed the good. Perhaps it is why I don't really think of myself today as a Harvard graduate but rather as L.A.'s Harvard hooker.

My mother and father fought from the earliest time I can recall. My mother was working while also trying to be a wife and mother. This was not an easy concept for a male chauvinist like my father to adapt to during the late sixties and early seventies. My dad was a successful entertainment attorney who represented people like Burt Reynolds and Ricky Nelson. He wanted my mother simply to be his wife and not pursue her own career, but she rebelled and after five tension-filled years finally left him.

My mother, my older brother, and I went from living

147

the comfortable Beverly Hills life to barely surviving on the verge of poverty, a struggling little family supported by a single working mother.

When I was still in grade school, a friend of my mother's called and offered her a job as a weatherperson in Michigan. We headed to the Midwest and Mom went on TV. She quickly moved up the ranks at her station to become weekend news anchorwoman. Not long after that she caught the eye of the people at NBC News and we moved again, this time to New York. I was thirteen. After a lot of sacrifices and hard work, my mom had finally made it, and I was very proud of her.

During this period my mom, my older brother, and I lived a comfortable Upper-East-Side-of-Manhattan life. I was sent off to boarding school, of course. The first school I went to was on a farm in the middle of nowhere, with twenty spoiled kids from the city. It was a super-strict school that, although coed, didn't allow boys and girls to see each other after 5 P.M. At first I was rebellious. I got caught making out with a boy, which in this school was a really bad offense. After a while, however, I got smarter and decided to cool the antics, becoming a good student rather than a misfit and troublemaker.

The following year I left this little boarding school and moved on to a really fine school. It was the beginning of the best years of my life.

Harvard Bound

The next boarding school I attended was one of the finest prep schools on the eastern seaboard. It is the kind of school that, if you perform well, almost ensures admission to the Ivy League universities. I went there for my four years of high school, and I did very well. We had classes on Saturdays, so I didn't go home very often on weekends. I loved being with the other kids—the whole environment was incredible.

When I was fifteen, my dad, who was still living in California and whom I saw only occasionally in the summers, told me that he wanted me to look up a boy at my school whose parents were family friends. I spotted this guy at school one day when he was standing with his friends, and I just popped into the middle of the group and said, "Hello." Immediately he knew who I was. "Oh, you're Jewel, whose dad is from California." That was the beginning of my first love affair. He and I were inseparable for the next two years.

My boyfriend was an all-American jock and honor student. We were both loved by the other kids and by the teaching staff. Mostly, though, we loved each other. We were best friends and lovers at this wonderful time in our lives, in this unreal setting of security and learning.

Although I was popular enough, I was not your typical prep school coed. I didn't have blond hair. I didn't come from Greenwich. My parents were divorced. I hardly knew my father (who wasn't a typical corporate executive like the other kids' fathers). I was Jewish, though I had never been raised to be religious. My boyfriend, who was from Los Angeles, was also a little different, and that was part of our bond. We mostly hung out with the artsy crowd, kids who were dancers and musicians. We were the serious types who wore black clothing while we planned our futures.

During the summer before my junior year, I decided that I was too young to be committed to one person. I felt like I needed to do other things and be with other people. When I returned to school that fall, I broke up with my boyfriend.

After that, I got very serious about my studies and hung out mostly with other girlfriends. I dated a Harvard football player for a short time, who turned out to be a total egotistical jerk. I never had a great deal of advice or support from either of my parents in the area of relationships. Not knowing how to handle things after a certain point, I usually broke up with guys who tried to get serious. The reward, perhaps, was that I was accepted as an undergraduate to Harvard University.

CAMBRIDGE, 1987–1991

A Family Tragedy

Harvard was a lot tougher than I thought it would be, but I lasted four years and graduated with a bachelor's degree in English in 1991. What made it particularly difficult was what happened to my mother during those years. She had been my best friend and my support system— really everything to me all my life. During my first year at the school, she lost her job at the network and not long afterward had a nervous breakdown. This made my college years very difficult emotionally as well as financially. I ended up on all kinds of student aid, and my father helped me, after I wrote him a ten-page letter pleading with him to do so.

My father had never really participated in my life. He didn't give my mother child support during all the years we were growing up. The financial pressure was all on her. Their divorce had been bitter, and they hardly spoke. Harvard was the only thing he ever came through on for me. I guess he was proud to have a daughter attending such a prestigious school.

By the time I was a senior, my mother's condition had deteriorated further. The loss of her job had completely frightened and depressed her. She had built her life around her career, and when it was suddenly over she simply couldn't handle it. She was institutionalized and given electroshock treatments numerous times. I loved my mother very much and it was awful to watch what was happening to her. She was never the same after that therapy.

My father attended my college graduation. It seemed strange. I hadn't seen him more than a few times in my twenty-three years of life, and here he was showing up at my graduation. My relationship with him had been limited to occasional summer vacations on the West Coast. He would buy me a beautiful dress, show me off as his summer princess, and then say, "So long. See you next time."

After the divorce, my father had built a whole life of his own filled with a new wife and new children. My stepmother was a very jealous, possessive woman who acted very cold toward me. She resented any attention I received from my father. When I visited their home, my stepmother made me sleep in the maid's room and forced me to eat at a different table from the rest of the family. I would sit in the kitchen with the maid eating leftovers, while the rest of the family was in the dining room.

My stepmother had my dad wrapped around her little finger. He would never even suggest that I join them at the table. My half brother and sister would ask why I couldn't eat with them, and neither my dad nor stepmother would answer them. It was bizarre, like something out of *Cinderella*.

During my years at Harvard, the family who had sustained me through childhood—my mother and my older brother—fell apart. My mother lost her mind, my brother became physically ill with an intestinal condition, and I just buried myself in my books, trying to survive and block out the pain. After graduation, I turned to my father, hoping to find family again with him.

A Harvard Grad Hits L.A.

*M*y dad invited me to come to California, and I hoped that this time it would be different. With my mother in a mental institution, I needed some security. I wanted to know that I had a bed to sleep in, food, clothing, and a chance to get started in life. I felt that moving to California was my best hope.

When I arrived I was pleased to discover that my dad was separated from his wife and had moved into a gorgeous new condo. I moved in with him. It was just the two of us and things were great at first. Then I started going to clubs—drinking, dancing, and partying, pretending that I was a rich, carefree Beverly Hills brat. I tried to be the party girl I never had the opportunity to be while in school. More than just making up for lost partying time, I think I was also running away from my mother's problems. Whatever the reason, my behavior made my father really angry, and he soon wanted me to move out.

As a graduation present, my father gave me a check for $25,000. The money was for whatever I needed—there were no strings attached, no budget, and no discussions on how to invest the money. This bright Harvard grad went out and bought clothes, took trips, and had fun with friends. I did some really stupid things. A psychologist later told me that I was angry because of what I had been through with my mother. It seems to me, though, that I was also angry that my father gave me money and not love. Neither of us, however, could talk about how we felt.

Even though my mother and father had never been on good terms before, he was very supportive of her after she was hospitalized. He arranged for her to be transferred from the institution in New York to one in Los Angeles, where we both visited her frequently. He provided money to help her and assured her that he would take care of anything she needed.

During this period I would get up around noon, go out shopping in my father's Jaguar, and perhaps make a feeble attempt to find a job. I had no idea what I wanted to do with my life. Studying had been the only thing I'd known while growing up. Now I couldn't decide what I had studied for. My father was very conflicted about my getting a job. On the one hand, he wanted to me to find myself, and on the other hand, he hadn't entirely let go of his old-fashioned chauvinist beliefs about women not belonging in the workplace.

At one point, I had an interview at the Teledyne Corporation. I was really gung ho about the prospective job and told everyone about it, including my stepmother. She was still trying to control my dad's life, even though they were separated. She kept asking me when the job would be starting, giving me the definite impression that she couldn't wait for me to go to work and move out of my father's home. I got so angry about what I thought was an attempt on her part to separate me from my father that I canceled the interview and, of course, never got the job. I felt as though my stepmother was trying to make me into the perfect little intellectual, Ivy League–educated, potential money-making stepdaughter, who was supposed to behave and perform in a certain way. She never had any idea who I really was, nor did she ever care to find out. I hated her and rebelled against everything she stood for.

After a few months I moved out of my father's condo to an apartment of my own. Things were just too tense. I still had what I hadn't yet squandered of the $25,000, and I took various menial types of jobs for money—promoting beer at the beach, telemarketing, selling art supplies, being an extra in movies—jobs that didn't require a college degree or even much of a brain.

I also gave acting a try and had a rude awakening about the manner in which women are regarded in Hollywood circles. On several commercial auditions I was given the well-known casting couch response—"I have this project, and I need to see what you look like in the nude." I'd say, "No, I don't think so. I won't compromise my integrity. I'm not that kind of girl." The next line would be, "Can you come back later tonight?"

Another line I often heard went something like, "I'm friends with Steven Seagal, and I could hook you up with him if you'll just treat me right." It didn't take a Harvard grad to realize that nothing much ever comes from those kinds of promises.

My family continued to get me down. It was almost Thanksgiving. My mother was in the mental hospital totally whacked out on lithium, and my father was growing more distant every day. I asked him if he was going to invite me over for Thanksgiving, and his only reply was that it wasn't a good time to have Thanksgiving.

I became so depressed that I took a bunch of sleeping pills and ended up in a mental hospital for the next ten days. While I was there I came to the realization that I was pretty much alone in life. My family was simply not going to be there for me. They wanted me to stay in the hospital—it was as though they thought I was following in my mother's footsteps.

It was nearing Christmas when I got out of the hospital, and the first thing my dad told me was that he, my stepmother, and their children were off to Hawaii for the holidays. I would have to fend for myself. That really, really hurt. At the time I didn't have a boyfriend; nor did I have any real friends to speak of. I started to hang out with a crowd of would-be actors, models, and hard-core partyers—pretty much all losers.

BEL AIR, SPRING 1992

From the Casting Couch to Nude Massage

A few months after my suicide attempt, I answered an ad for dancers that one of my loser friends showed me. I arrived at a Bel Air estate in a really nice family neighborhood. When I entered the house, I found a bunch of beautiful nude girls walking around. It was a massage parlor owned by a guy, David, who hired pretty college girls to do massages in the nude for male patrons.

My interview consisted of David telling me to take my clothes off and lie down. He said he wanted to show me how to do it. Well, I wasn't stupid. I knew what he was going to show me. I told him that the job was not exactly what I had in mind and started to leave. Before I left, however, one of the girls came over to me and gave me the lowdown. "It's really easy. All you have to do is run your fingers from the guy's neck to his toes and massage outward. Don't let him touch you, just do the massage. There's a bodyguard in the kitchen with a gun so you can scream if anything happens. When you're done, David will collect the money, and if you're good, the guy will give you a tip."

I asked the woman for a little more detail. I knew there had to be more. She continued, "These guys will ask for a lot of things, but we're not allowed to do it. Just say no thank you, try to act sexy, and keep massaging." Finally she admitted to the bottom line. "There is one thing called a 'release,' where you jerk the guy off by hand. You can do that, but not real sex."

The clients in David's Bel Air House of Massage were everything from Japanese and American businessmen to police and FBI agents looking for a thrill. David even had a few celebrity clients. A lot of guys pretended that they had no idea the girls would be doing the massage in the nude. They claimed they were just coming to have their shoulders rubbed to relieve tension after a hard day of work. Sure.

Clients paid $80 for a half-hour nude massage. The girl would get to keep $30 of that, and she might get another $20, $40, $60, or even $100 tip, if the guy was feeling generous. I ended up working two eight-hour shifts a week for David and making anywhere from $100 to $500 a shift. We didn't entertain the men, serve them drinks, or anything like that. They just came for the massage and left. In between clients, I'd read a book.

There were four or five girls working at David's at any

given time. The neighbors didn't seem to care, even though I'm sure they must have noticed all the pretty girls and men entering and leaving the house. I guess that in L.A. this sort of coming and going is perfectly normal. I worked for David about four months before he fired me for refusing to give him head, or whatever he wanted, like the other girls were doing.

SAN DIEGO AND THE
HOLLYWOOD HILLS, 1992

From Nude Massage to a Sugar Daddy

By now I had gone through the entire $25,000 that my father had given me after my college graduation. I had also found the working world to be less than rewarding, especially my four months at David's Bel Air House of Massage. The next thing I did was stumble across a sugar daddy who took me in.

I met an Arab man who produced nude Playboy-type videos. He first hired me as a choreographer for one of his videos—a perfect way, I thought, to use my years of ballet training. My Arab friend lived in a mansion by the sea in San Diego, and I soon became his girlfriend, though I'm sure not the only one.

I told my Arab friend that I needed to be supported, and he agreed to pay for my clothes and other living expenses, just as a father would. I was expected to cook, do errands, and keep his house in order. I suppose I was really looking for a surrogate father since my relationship with my own father had always been so difficult.

Unlike my father, this sugar daddy was only about ten years older than me, but he was just as controlling and domineering as if he were thirty years older. Though at first I thought the arrangement was what I wanted, it didn't take long before I grew unhappy with it. I kept thinking about how I had tried to satisfy my father and win his approval and love, and here I was doing it again for a man I really didn't even care for.

I told my sugar daddy that I needed to live in L.A. and eventually convinced him to rent me a house in Laurel Canyon and keep me on staff as a choreographer for his nude videos. He stayed with me on weekends and returned to San Diego during the week. I knew that continuing with this guy was the wrong path, but I didn't know what else to do or where else to go.

Our arrangement became unglued when a neighbor told my friend that other men were coming to the house in his absence. Actually, I had started seeing another guy, but only one—someone most people would label a total loser. He had long hair and smoked and sold weed all day long. I found him totally attractive at that point in my life.

My apologies, pleas, and explanations didn't matter to my surrogate father/sugar-daddy keeper. His ego was badly damaged. He called me a whore, kicked me out, emptied the Laurel Canyon house, and put everything—the furniture, my clothes, the dishes, my personal mementos—into storage. I had nothing and nowhere to go.

NORTH HOLLYWOOD, WINTER 1993

Living in a Porno Flick House

I called up one of the girls with whom I had worked in the massage parlor to see if I could stay with her. She was unwilling to share her one-bedroom apartment but suggested I call another David—not Mr. Massage Parlor—who lived in a big house in the Valley.

I called David number two, an Englishman, and met him at his house in North Hollywood. He seemed totally natural and normal and invited me to stay, showing me an empty bedroom. It didn't occur to me that a total stranger inviting you to live with him was at all abnormal.

On the second day I learned what was up. This David filmed porno movies in his house. He told me that I could either sit on the couch and watch or, as he said in his English accent, "You could be in them, luv!" I was stunned and told him that I didn't want to be in his movies.

Ever since I had moved out of my father's condo, I had felt very weird and isolated. Soon after I was gone, my stepmother reconciled with my dad and apparently convinced him that I was a no-good thief intent on robbing them. My father had hit me a few times when I lived with him, but rather than admit he was wrong, he tried to blame me. My father obtained a restraining order prohibiting me from coming near them. I called my older brother and asked for help but even he was less than cordial to me.

It was all so bizarre. I was supposed to be the good little girl, but when I didn't do everything my family wanted I became the scapegoat. In an attempt to reconcile, I wrote my dad an emotional letter asking for forgiveness. I expressed my love for him and my hope that we could again be father and daughter. After he received my letter, he invited me to dinner with him and my brother.

At dinner he told me that he had heard from a policeman he knew that I was working in porno films. I was in total shock. I told him that I wasn't doing porno—I had just moved into a house where they did porno movies because I had nowhere else to go right now. He also knew about the nude videos I had worked on with my Arab boyfriend. It angered me that he obviously had someone spying on me, but I tried to explain to him that I had just done what I needed to do to survive.

That night, my father asked me if I needed anything. I told him I could use $5,000 so I could get my life in order, find a place, and try to find legitimate work. He told me he didn't have that kind of money. I knew he was lying—he had tons of money. I told him thanks anyway and left. It was the last time I saw him that year. I felt like I had been abandoned by my last resort. I was feeling depressed and very desperate.

I continued to live in the house of porn in North Hollywood and finally started doing what my father had accused me of doing—I became an actress in porno movies. When you're desperate enough, you take what you can get. It was the most degrading, humiliating, low-life, scummy, and scary situation I've ever been in.

I was kind of drawn in by the camaraderie among the small community of porno actors. I seemed to always be seeking some kind of family and, at that time, this was the best I could do. We'd all go out together at night for drinks and share wonderful lunches during the day. And, of course, everybody was sleeping with everybody else all the time.

Most of the other women were strippers, many of whom worked at the Hollywood Tropicana. The majority were really beautiful blondes. One had three kids, even though she was barely twenty years old. I couldn't believe I was in this crowd. For the most part, the people who work in porn are isolated, desperate people—people without family and certainly without much self-esteem. When you expose your genitals to the world, you have to be a very scared and defensive person.

Most of the time I hid my background from everyone, but even though the majority of my peers were lower-class and uneducated, we had a lot in common. I may not have been a model or a weight trainer with a grade school education, but I, too, was alone, without family, and very angry and defensive.

My stage name was Jennifer Jewel, and my films were sold in the sleaziest porno shops in the Valley. I was never a star, only a scene actress. You get paid per scene in porno films, which is really a polite term for a "come shot." I would generally do three scenes a day, earning about $200 per scene. The stars of porno make a whole lot more, but it's not easy to become a porno star. You really have to work at it.

At one point I almost had a chance to become a porno star. Another English guy I met at David's house, Stick Nasty, invited me to go to England with him to make films there. Mr. Nasty said he had been a millionaire once, back in jolly old England, and together we would make millions again. He was the scum of the earth, but I was ready to leave the country with him.

Then one of the other "scene" players moved into the house, a seventeen-year-old female drug addict who hated me instantly. It may have been because she was jealous that I was in a movie she wasn't cast in, but I don't really know. What I do know is that she stole half of my things, and when I confronted her, she got really pissed off and denied it. Later I was away for a few days and returned to find that she had stolen the rest of my things. What was left she'd thrown out onto the front lawn. She had also been very busy moving in on my territory with Stick Nasty. He had already left for England without me.

I had lost my belongings and was once more out on the street. I was actually homeless this time, living in a white 1978 Pontiac that my Arab friend had bought me and for some reason hadn't repossessed.

BEVERLY HILLS, SPRING 1993

Homeless

I drove around in a state of total depression. On one cold and windy day, I rested my overheated Pontiac in front of a really nice home in Beverly Hills. I had no idea what I was going to do. I thought whatever happens will happen. I was beyond reason.

A woman who lived in the house I parked in front of was staring at me through the window. I thought she was going to call the police, but instead she came over to my car to see if I was all right and to ask if I needed anything. I said, "No, it's okay. I don't need anything." She could tell, however, that I was quite distraught. "Let me call your family or a shelter," she offered. I continued to resist her kindness, and she finally went back into her house and returned with a blanket and a check for $120. I touched the fabric of the blanket. The fine, soft cloth seemed so beautiful to me, and the $120 was like a million dollars.

I went to her bank in Beverly Hills, cashed the check,

and then checked into a motel room for a shower and some sleep. As I lay in that room, I was in a daze. I couldn't believe that I was really homeless. How could I be the only person in the history of my family who was ever homeless? It was impossible. I was angry and frightened by the situation I was in.

I had picked up a copy of a newspaper called the *L.A. Express*, basically a porno paper. It was a far cry from the classifieds of the *New York Times*, but I knew the territory because my Arab sugar daddy had often leafed through this paper looking for models to be in his adult films. I called up about five or six pimps from various ads that read "Nude Girls Wanted" or something similar. I knew the drill.

Two of the guys called me back while I was still at the motel. One of them was English, and since I had developed this fondness for English men, I set up an appointment with him for the next day.

NORTH HOLLYWOOD, 1993

My First Pimp

The English guy arrived promptly at my motel the following morning. As soon as he saw me he announced that he was going to change my life. His name was Tim. He was around thirty-five, and was half English, half Indian. He lived with his mother somewhere in the Valley. The first thing Tim did was rent a nice furnished apartment for me down the hall from his place in North Hollywood. He acted like he was my mother—cooked for me, did whatever I wanted, and seemed to really care for me. Every morning he would come over to check up on me. Then he'd stop by again every night. At first we'd just have dinner or go to a movie. Then I started working for him. He was, after all, a pimp.

Tim's clients were not terrific, even though to hear him talk, they were all exceptional men. Some of them were downright low-life crooks. But most were just sleazy Valley businessmen who were cheating on their wives and girlfriends. I only saw one celebrity through Tim, tennis player Bjorn Borg.

I stayed with Tim, working for him and living in his Valley apartment for about a year and a half. He was using me, of course, but he also was good and kind to me, as no one I had met since I left my father's had been. He could have said, "Do your tricks and stay at some motel. Just pay me my cut." Instead, he protected me and took me under his wing. For his protection, he got 40 percent of the take. He charged as much as the traffic would bear, anywhere from $200 to $600 a trick.

I worked a lot—two or more tricks per day for six days a week, with only Sundays off. He also had a couple of ex–porno star girls working for him, so he was doing okay financially off of us.

At that point in my life I didn't know or really care that hookers on the other side of the hill, in Hollywood and Beverly Hills, were making three or four times as much money. I was just trying to survive and stay out of danger. It may sound ridiculous, but I rationalized that I was less likely to be arrested in the Valley. The johns were paying less so I figured there would be less chance of trouble. In reality, however, I now realize that it was probably more dangerous where I was working because I was dealing with a lower class of clientele.

THE SAN FERNANDO VALLEY, 1993

My Worst Trick

*O*ne client Tim sent me to was a young guy who lived in a really cute house in the Valley. It was a small but very beautiful place. The guy was a real estate agent who was barely twenty years old. I couldn't understand how he had made so much money at such a young age.

The guy was very overweight—almost obese. He wanted oral sex, but I just couldn't do it. I was totally grossed out because of his weight, I guess, and I just panicked. He got really angry and shoved my head down on the pillow so hard that I couldn't breathe, almost suffocating me.

I lay there for a minute, playing dead. I was afraid that any reaction at all would make him even more angry. When he finally got up I pocketed my money and got out of there fast. The guy actually called me again—the wackos always do—but I never went back. Even I had some limits.

WEST HOLLYWOOD, 1994

No Love with Bjorn Borg

*T*im called me one day to tell me that he had a surprise client for me. He wouldn't say who it was until we got to the hotel, which was, for a change, not in the Valley.

We took Tim's BMW to the Bel Age Hotel in West Hollywood. He waited in the hotel lobby while I went up to the suite of the surprise client—tennis star Bjorn Borg. Borg's manager was there, as well as a beautiful blond girl who looked like Christie Brinkley but who was coked out and oblivious. It was very sad to see this once great tennis player, now past his prime, snorting coke up his nose with hookers in a hotel room.

Borg was in town for some celebrity tournament, and I was part of his pre-play celebration. The Christie Brinkley look-alike turned out to be a stripper, and she did her thing. Then I took off my coat to reveal that I was wearing just lingerie, a garter, stockings, and high heels, as instructed by Tim. Another hooker showed up at some point who was a real low-life street-hooker type.

I was really in a zombie mood, sort of spaced out as though I weren't even there. I would often just zone out and kind of play the prostitute—acting sexy but not really being into it. It was just a room filled with empty, bored people trying to get the feeling going, myself included.

Borg also appeared to be in zombieland. He just seemed to be going through the motions, trying to accommodate his manager who had been thoughtful enough to arrange for the stripper and the hookers for Borg's late-night entertainment.

Finally the manager went into one bedroom with the street hooker, and I went into the other with Borg. The stripper just did more drugs and smoked cigarettes in the living room. Borg and I didn't actually have sex. I just watched him jerk off, and then I pretended to jerk off myself. He couldn't have cared less or been less involved. He seemed to just want it over, and so did I. All I could think of was getting out of there.

I ended up making $300 that night. Tim took his 40 percent cut and we left. Tim told me he would call Borg and his manager in a couple of days to see if we could be of further service, but it never happened. They left town and I'm sure poor old Bjorn was just as glad.

Jewel

HOLLYWOOD, 1994

A Hollywood Agent Who Bargained for Sex

*C*harlie Sheen's manager, whose name is Brent, was a client of mine. Brent liked me to come over and spank him, whip him, or drip candle wax on him, all while pretending I was getting off. He would lie in bed or on the couch and masturbate himself to climax.

Brent was a pretty easy job, but he never seemed to have much money. A lot of agents and managers I saw claimed they didn't have much cash, even though they all had fancy leased cars and the right clothes. To make up for his cash-flow problems, Brent used to pay me in durable goods. One time he offered me his TV set. I took it. A few weeks later I spent an hour with him, and when we were done he announced that it was *The Price Is Right* time again—I could take something else from his home. I chose another appliance, a microwave, I think. By the time I stopped seeing Brent, I had pretty much stripped his apartment bare.

NORTH HOLLYWOOD, 1994

Out on My Own Again

*A*fter the Bjorn Borg visit, Tim had a few aspirations of breaking ground with famous, higher-paying clients. Ultimately, however, all he really ended up doing was making a decent living as a pimp. Ironically, Tim is now an executive with IBM. He's a good salesman—only the product has changed.

167

All the while I was working for him, Tim had been living with his mother in a modest apartment a few doors down from mine. Tim's mother seemed to take a blind eye to everything that was going on. She probably knew, but maybe not. As long as there was money for food and rent, I don't think she asked too many questions. He told her that he had a sales and marketing job, which, of course, was one of those believable half-truths. Tim was a really fine liar.

Tim's mother never liked me much, but one day she really flipped out and decided that I should leave. I'm not sure what set her off. All I know is that she started screaming at me, calling me a bad girl who was the cause of all the trouble in her son's life. Of course, this bad girl was also paying her rent and feeding her.

She actually called the police to have me thrown out of the apartment. While they were there and I was packing up my stuff, she said, ominously, to the officers, "I know all the things she does." Fortunately they didn't care, and I wasn't arrested. If she only knew what a can of worms she was about to open—and if I was arrested, then her precious boy would have been, too.

STUDIO CITY, 1995

Even Hookers Get Raped

I found a new place to live—a nice apartment in Studio City—and a new madam, whose name was Charlie. At one time Charlie had been a successful real estate broker, but when I first met her she was making more money selling women than houses. Like in the television show

Charlie's Angels, Charlie called her working girls her "angels." Also like in the show, I never actually met Charlie. She was just a voice on the phone from somewhere in the Valley. Her girls didn't know where she was or who she was. We only knew what she wanted us to do and when.

I became friends for a time with Elizabeth, another girl who worked for Charlie. Elizabeth was from South Carolina, and she was very sweet. I considered her my best friend, but it's difficult for prostitutes to have real friendships with one another. If you've been in the business for more than a month, you hate yourself and therefore, on some level, hate anyone else who's into it, too.

Elizabeth started dating this guy, Steve Stevens, who was Billy Idol's former guitarist and songwriting partner. I went over to visit her at his apartment one day. We hung out for a while and watched videos. Then Elizabeth and Steve started having sex, and I watched. She was sucking him off or something equally disgusting and boring. Afterward Elizabeth wanted me to sleep over. I didn't really want to, but Steve gave me some pills that he said would help me sleep. They must have been heavy-duty barbiturates because my head hit the pillow, and I was out. When I woke up, Steve was on top of me, fucking me, while Elizabeth was in the other room passed out.

Later, when Elizabeth woke up, she and I left together and went out to lunch. I didn't say anything to her about what her boyfriend had done, but I felt bad about it. I went home and showered, and she went back to his place. That afternoon Charlie, the madam, called me with a job. I told her that I was really tired and didn't feel well. She said that I didn't sound like myself and wanted to know what had happened.

I told her the whole thing and she said, "You know, Jewel, you were raped." I muttered that I was there willingly, and maybe I was responsible somehow, but she insisted, "No, you were raped." She told me that I should go back to the apartment, tell Elizabeth, and confront Steve.

When I did what Charlie suggested, Elizabeth flipped out. She screamed, "Why are you doing this to me?" Stunned, I retorted, "It happened to me! I'm not doing it to you!" Steve claimed that I had dragged him into the bathroom and had been coming on to him. I told her that he was lying, but no matter what I said, she didn't want to believe me. I was ruining her fantasy of being a rock star's girlfriend.

Even though it ended my friendship with Elizabeth, I'm glad I confronted the guy. As a prostitute, I didn't really think that I could be raped or that I deserved to be treated decently when it came to sex. Charlie thought I did deserve respect, and I listened to her. It helped me a little. Every shred of self-respect helps.

STUDIO CITY, 1995

L.A. Express Girl

I continued to work for Charlie for a while. She had a decent class of clients. One guy I saw was Todd, the former manager of a major league baseball team. He was married, with kids my age, and was a pleasant enough guy.

Like most "escorts," however, I resented having to pay the commission to my madam and figured I could make more money by setting up calls myself. I began looking for some business on the side by advertising in *L.A. Express*. A lot of prostitutes do it. They put their picture in the paper—

just their body, without their face, and list their pager number. A working girl who gets business this way has to be careful, however. She has to know how to weed out the cops and the wackos.

When a hooker finds business from an ad, it's also a good idea for her to hire a driver to take her to the calls—and to wait outside in case anything goes wrong. For a small cut, a working girl in L.A. can hire guys who are struggling actors or musicians or ex-bodyguards. It took me a while to learn all of this, however, and not before I got slapped around and stiffed by johns a few times.

One time, after a guy hit me and refused to pay me, I called up Charlie for help. She scolded me for advertising in the porno newspaper. "Scum people are in that paper. What were you thinking? You could have been killed!"

I was forced to use *L.A. Express* for all my business after a while, however, because one day Charlie suddenly disappeared. No one knows what happened to her. I guess that either she suspected cops were on to her, or she had to go on the run from her abusive ex-husband. Whatever the reason, that was the end of Charlie.

It didn't take long for me to learn how to handle things myself. I found plenty of clients from *L.A. Express*, including about twenty lawyers and twenty doctors. Of course, like every other hooker in this town, I had lots of clients who worked in the entertainment industry.

WESTWOOD, 1995

The CAA Agent

*O*ne client who answered my ad in *L.A. Express* was an agent at Creative Artists Agency, CAA, one of the biggest and most powerful talent agencies in the movie business. He sounded normal when he called and asked me to come over to his place in Westwood at 2 A.M. one night. When I arrived, however, it was a scene out of a weird movie. Everything in the house was black leather. The agent was shirtless, sitting on his black leather couch in front of a coffee table that held a truckload of cocaine. Another guy, who looked like a *GQ* model, was also there.

We all snorted a few lines of coke. I rarely did drugs except with clients. My mom was so out of control that drugs scare me. But clients usually wanted me to partake with them so I would. After we did the coke, the agent asked me to undress and I performed a little strip number for them. Then the agent and I went into his bedroom, leaving the *GQ* guy in the other room watching TV and doing more coke.

It was a long sexual evening, lasting probably four hours. The guy had a very small penis, and I guess guys who do coke all have trouble getting off. After it was finally over, he wanted me to sleep over, then spend the next few days in Tahoe with him and the *GQ* guy. I didn't want to and politely said I had to leave.

This agent called me about five times after that. Once he said he had a client who was in town from the Middle East. He wanted me to get a girlfriend and go out with the two of them. I turned him down. I didn't feel like dealing with his drugs and his tiny cock anymore. He may have been a powerful agent, but he was just too weird for me.

HOLLYWOOD, 1995

L'eeza Gibbons's Producer

*A*nother client I met through *L.A. Express* was a guy who told me he was the producer of Leeza Gibbons's TV show. He was really strange. At first he was very secretive. I had to meet him a block away from his apartment and then walk to the door with him. When we got inside, his demeanor changed, and he was very friendly. He offered me champagne and we talked, or rather he did. He told me what a big producer he was and how many celebrities he knew. Then he put on a porno movie, which we watched for a while before he asked me to go into the bedroom.

He couldn't seem to get excited, however. Once again I think it might have been because of cocaine. I hadn't seen him do any, but perhaps he had some before I arrived. Finally he lay down on the bed and asked me to walk on him in my high heels. I did and that finally got him off.

He called me a few more times. On one call, he bragged that he could get me photographed for *Playboy* magazine. I didn't know whether to believe anything he was saying, so I called the people at *Leeza* and asked if he worked there. They said he was the executive producer, so at least some of what he had been saying was true. I never got that *Playboy* shoot, however.

SANTA MONICA, FALL 1995

A Paramount Executive Answers My Ad

*Y*et another guy I met through my *L.A. Express* ad was an executive at Paramount Studios, a guy named Stan.

173

I met him at his rather modest house in Santa Monica. He was a really good-looking guy, but he had a bad drug habit. He did coke and speed all the time.

We hit it off that first night, and I ended up spending the whole weekend with him. I quit charging him and became his girlfriend, and we were soon spending every weekend together. He was best friends with one of Heidi Fleiss's former girls and knew her whole crowd. We would go out and party with these former Heidi girls, though I never met the great ex-madam herself.

The worst drug experience I ever had was because of one of the girls who had worked for Heidi. We were at a club in Hollywood, and she slipped me four Ecstasy pills which I stupidly took. I had a horrible reaction. First I began to grind my teeth together so hard that I thought I would break my jaw. Then my legs began to spasm, as though I was having an epileptic fit. I was totally freaked out, and I thought the stuff would never wear off.

My relationship with this movie executive ended because I introduced him to my former friend Elizabeth. She turned him against me, but I don't really mind. She can have him. His drug habit makes him a really pathetic guy. If people like him are deciding which movies get made, no wonder there's not much worth seeing out there.

SAN DIEGO, 1996

More Family Tragedies

During all this time I had been almost completely cut off from my family. I tried to contact my father once after a guy I was dating beat me up. It was a big mistake. He took my phone call, but it was like talking to a robot, like I wasn't even his daughter. He told me I made him sick.

Then another tragedy occurred. My dad and stepmother had moved into a house in La Costa, north of San Diego, and there was some problem with a radiation leak in or near the house. They got some sort of radiation poisoning, to the point where everyone's hair was falling out. My father wanted to move but my stepmother, who cares more about money than anything else, wanted to stay until they could command a better price for the house. One year later, in 1994, my half brother developed a brain tumor and died. He was only nineteen. Of course, my stepmother claimed that the radiation poisoning had nothing to do with my half brother's death, but that's not my version of the story.

My father was really distraught over my half brother's death. He had been having a lot of health problems himself. He suffered from diabetes and had to have one of his kidneys removed. During the surgery, however, the doctor cut a vein he wasn't supposed to, and my father ended up losing both kidneys and going on dialysis. I wanted to visit him in the hospital after the surgery, but my stepmother told me that she would have me arrested if I did. I went anyway, but my father was so medicated that he didn't seem to know me.

My father's health kept deteriorating. My stepmother moved him out of their house, into an apartment in San Diego, and hired a nurse to take care of him. He was in a wheelchair and was on medication, though he was often lucid. I would drive down to visit him when I could, and my stepmother would always find out and ask me to leave.

Finally I guess everything was just too much for him. My father blew his brains out. He left a note to the family saying that he didn't want to go on and asking us for forgiveness. In the note he said he didn't want to live any-more without his son, and he was sorry he couldn't com-municate with me.

My stepmother never told anyone outside the family that my father had killed himself. She was such a phony. I also think she destroyed my father's will. The only thing, supposedly, that he left was a scribbled note, written in the last two months of his life, leaving everything to her except for 1 percent each to me and my older brother. My father was a lawyer. I know he would have written a will, and I believe he would have left his children more.

I invited my mother to his funeral, but she acted very goofy, embarrassing everyone. She now lives in a one-room apartment in the Valley. She has no money and is a shadow of her former self. I don't really have much of a relationship with her. It's hard to. I feel like she's just waiting to die.

I have a cordial relationship with my older brother, but he's got his own problems and really is not there for me. Once again, I'm very aware, as I was after I tried to commit suicide five years ago, that I am truly on my own.

ENCINO, 1996

Where I Am Today

*M*y mother won two major awards as a broadcaster. My dad whose parents were Holocaust survivors, was a successful Beverly Hills entertainment attorney. I am a Harvard graduate. Now, at fifty, my mother is broke, and plagued with mental illness. My father committed suicide at fifty-five. I am an ex-hooker at twenty-eight and have no idea what the future holds for me. I don't know what went wrong with all of us.

I feel as though I am living in a dead zone right now. I have stopped turning tricks and am living off my small inheritance and what money I've saved. I have a lot of anger and resentment toward my family, and I know that my anger is keeping me from going on with my life in any productive way. Still, I don't know how to forgive any of them.

I'm also really weirded out about men. I hope someday to be able to have a normal man in my life and not a sicko who is just looking for a self-destructive person to party with. I'm not sure that, after what I've been through, I will be able to trust any man. But I hope I can. I also hope that a man exists who will be able to respect and trust me.

It seems unfair that most people look down so severely on the women involved in prostitution but not on the men. People call us whores and think of us as the scum of the earth. Because men are in control in society, people too often turn a blind eye to the same kind of behavior from men. President Clinton's campaign adviser Dick Morris might have been fired because of a prostitution scandal, but he was also offered a several million dollar book contract. Men like to be serviced sexually by prostitutes, and why not? They don't have to suffer the same kind of stigma and consequences, if any, that the prostitutes do.

It was only six months ago that my father died. I guess when you are confronted with death, particularly a parent's death, you start to think more about what is important in life and about spiritual things. I believe the one thing that his death has given me is a faith in God, which is kind of weird for me. I never thought much about God before. I believe now that God must have spared me for a reason. I don't know yet what that reason is, but I hope that someday it will be for something good.

177

PART THREE

Hollywood Hopefuls

Jennifer Young and Tatiana Thumbtzen come from opposite worlds. Jennifer, the quintessential Beverly Hills blonde, is the daughter of actor Gig Young and prominent Beverly Hills realtor Elaine Young. Tatiana, the dark-eyed biracial brunette, is the adopted daughter of middle-class schoolteacher parents from Clearwater, Florida.

But Jennifer, the singer and actress, and Tatiana, the dancer and actress, have something in common. They have both been chasing the Hollywood dream, spending years of their lives trying to reach success in show business. Along the way they've encountered distractions, disappointments, and disillusionment. They've met their share of famous men and women. Fortunately, neither has succumbed to the temptation of prostitution, as the others in this book have or as three of the young women in *You'll Never Make Love in This Town Again* did. Their good fortune, however, didn't come from lack of opportunity.

Like gamblers who flock to Las Vegas and Atlantic City, women like Tatiana arrive in Hollywood every day, all clinging tightly to their dreams of stardom. Already here are the children of the famous stars of the past, many of whom are also hoping to achieve the heights of success that their parents attained. But whether they come from Tinseltown royalty or are peasants from the hinterlands, they soon learn that it's hard to navigate the Hollywood highway to stardom. There are many dangers and many dead-ends along the way.

Jennifer and Tatiana reveal stories of the Hollywood they've encountered, of the many famous and infamous people they have known, and of the obstacles they, like other Hollywood hopefuls, have faced in the pursuit of their dreams.

Pauline Kael, the film critic, once said, "You can die of hope in Hollywood." Whether Jennifer's or Tatiana's hopes will be fatal to either of them remains to be seen. Certainly, though, they've each had their share of pain, along with some joy. Here are their stories, uncensored and . . . with feeling.

Tatiana

HEIGHT:	*5'7"*
HAIR:	*Brunette*
EYES:	*Brown*
WEIGHT:	*105*
PROFESSION:	*Model and actress*
BORN:	*Clearwater, Florida*
HOBBIES:	*Writing and horseback riding*
EDUCATION:	*New York School for Professional Children*
FIRST SEXUAL EXPERIENCE:	*At nineteen, in New York, with first real boyfriend*
GOALS & DESIRES:	*To be a working actress, find the man of my dreams, and get married*
SEXUAL FANTASY:	*To find my soulmate*
DRUGS:	*None*
HAPPIEST MEMORY:	*Receiving the key to the city of Clearwater*
WORST EXPERIENCE:	*Seeing Sheryl Crow dressed like me and taking my place in the BAD tour.*
DEALS/DATES/ ENCOUNTERS:	*Harry Belafonte, Jerry Buss, Robert De Niro, Prince, Billy Dee Williams, Michael Jackson*

CLEARWATER, FLORIDA, AND NEW YORK CITY

Dreams and Opportunities

My father, O'Cain Thumbtzen, was an elementary school principal. My mother, Evelyn, was an art teacher. The Thumbtzens were actually my adopted parents, but they are and always will be my true family. My adopted parents' heritage is a melting pot of Irish and American Indian on my father's side and Cherokee on my mother's side. My own heritage is a combination of African American on my biological mother's side and Anglo-Cuban on my biological father's side.

I grew up in Clearwater, Florida, on the Gulf Coast, in a middle-class black community. We lived in a very nice two-story Spanish-style home with a pool. My biracial background was never a day-to-day dilemma for me because I lived in a loving home. In the bigger world, however, things were tough.

At school I often felt like an oddball. I didn't relate to a lot of the other kids and was frequently taunted—by other blacks, in particular—because of my looks. Once, a black girl who was much bigger than me shoved me and said, "You ain't black, you ain't white. Just what color are you?" "I'm the color you see I am," I answered as I looked into her menacing face, afraid of what was coming next.

She hated my answer. She pushed me against the wall and pulled my hair, screaming at me, "Don't be a smart-ass!"

My family gave me a wonderful sense of security. From them I learned moral values and a sense of right and wrong, which would help me immensely later in the Hollywood jungle. I had two older brothers and one sister. They were already out of the house and on their own when I came along. Being the baby, I was a little spoiled by my protective parents.

Television brought the world of show business into our home. I was enthralled by the singing and dancing on the variety shows and in old movies. I remember loving the Jackson 5, and particularly the little one, Michael, when I saw them perform on "The Ed Sullivan Show." Little did I know then that I would one day meet the Jacksons and that, they would have a tremendous impact on my life.

I loved watching Fred Astaire and Ginger Rogers, and also Gene Kelly, especially in *Singing in the Rain*. Shirley MacLaine was another all-time favorite. When I grew up, I wanted to be a dancer like these wonderful performers.

Television also opened my eyes to the world of ballet. I was mesmerized at age six when I first saw Violette Verdy and Edward Villella on "The Ed Sullivan Show." Their dancing was the most beautiful movement I had ever seen.

"Mommy, Mommy, I want to be a ballerina," I pleaded. My mother bought me children's books on ballet, and I devoured them, committing every word and every image to memory. I began to mimic ballet positions. I lived for anything having to do with music and dance. This did not make me any more popular with the other kids in school. A biracial ballerina was not on anyone's Top Ten list of most easily understood and most popular kids. But at the time it didn't matter that much to me.

When I was eight, my mother enrolled me in a small,

local ballet academy run by Beatriz De Paris, an instructor of the Balanchine school. After I proudly displayed my knowledge of ballet positions, she said she could tell that I had talent. And there was no question that I had the desire.

In dance class I made my first real, close friend. Her name was Marion, and we had absolutely everything in common. It was wonderful to finally have a close friend and to not feel so much like an outsider anymore.

By the time I was ten, I went on my toes. Normally, it takes three to four years for a beginning dancer to go en pointe, but I couldn't wait to get my first pair of pointe shoes. That same year my dance idol Violette Verdy came to Clearwater and attended a performance at the school. She singled out me and my best friend, Marion, and told my teacher that we had great talent. "I will follow their work," she said.

Verdy returned to Clearwater two years later and offered me the opportunity to audition for the School of American Ballet in New York, which was the feeder school for the NYC Ballet Company.

At thirteen I traveled to New York City with my mother. I was awestruck, scared, and excited, all at the same time. On that first day in the city I witnessed a homeless man who had been hit by a car and left to bleed in the gutter. He was lying in the street, and no one would help him. To this day I've never forgotten that moment. During my first night there, at the Barbizon Hotel, I kept waking up and talking to my mother about the man. I couldn't stop crying.

The next day proved more positive. On the way to dance class, my mother and I saw a film being shot on the streets of New York. It was *Taxi Driver* with Robert De Niro, whom I would run into again under very different circumstances many years later. One of the crew approached us and asked if we wanted to be extras in the film. It was an exciting proposition for a thirteen-year-old from a small town, particularly one who had spent every breathing moment of her young life dreaming of and planning a career in show business.

To my horror my mother turned down the offer. We had to get to the dance academy, which was, after all, why we were in New York. Surviving the disappointment of not appearing in *Taxi Driver*, I arrived at the dance studio to face an even greater opportunity.

I was offered a full scholarship to the School of American Ballet. Talk about big changes in a little life! The grant would enable me to attend the most prestigious dance school in the country and begin serious, professional training. To me, this was a dream come true. A woman I had seen at age six on "The Ed Sullivan Show" was now hand-picking me to become her protégée.

When my mother and I returned home to Clearwater, my family and the community were buzzing. My parents and I had several lengthy discussions over the next few weeks. They were trying to talk themselves into, or out of, approving this major step in my life. In the end, they realized it was the opportunity of a lifetime, and they let me go.

In New York I lived with Violette Verdy and her mother on Eighty-fifth Street and West End Avenue. She took care of me and three other girls who were attending the school. Cicely Tyson happened to be a neighbor in our building. I'd often see her in the elevator with her dog. At first I was too shy to speak to her. Finally I got up the courage to talk, telling her how adorable her dog was. Cicely just ignored me, and I was crushed. But I was learning that this was New York City, not Clearwater. People behaved differently in the big city than they did in our small community at home.

I worked very hard at the dance academy. I'd often stay after school just to watch other advanced classes. I wanted to absorb everything I possibly could. I'd watch the men's classes, the women's classes, and the rehearsals. I'd study everyone.

The great dancers of the world often dropped in at the academy. Nureyev appeared quite often to rehearse and sometimes even took my classes. It was awesome to watch the great dancer fly through the rarefied air in his white tights.

The first summer I was in New York, Baryshnikov took a class I was in. I first saw him as he stretched and did his warm-ups. All of us were awestruck. "What is he doing taking one of my classes?" I wondered. Then, as I was beginning to do my own warm-up, he walked over to me with a big grin on his face. I was all flustered. He flirted with me a bit, but I didn't have a clue how to respond. I was, after all, just thirteen.

NEW YORK CITY, 1979

Failing in Love at Nineteen

Through most of my teen years, boys were just dance partners, no more. I had been very sheltered, both at home and living under Violette's care. Dating wasn't an option for me. It wasn't a part of my existence, and frankly I didn't think much about it. I was nineteen before I had my first boyfriend.

One day I was in Central Park with some friends from the dance academy, and I saw a very athletic guy with long black hair playing Frisbee. He was gorgeous. I remember admiring his beauty and agility as he jumped and turned and twirled through the air. Even though he wasn't a dancer, he had the same kind of grace.

He saw me watching him and came over and introduced himself. His name was Johnny, and he was from Chile. We dated for a couple of weeks before we were intimate. He was very loving—always caressing, kissing, and showering me with affection and attention. For a first love, it was a great experience. We stayed together for a year and a half, but it was during a major transition in my life, both personally and professionally. Though he was wonderful, I was young and had other roads to travel.

NEW YORK CITY, 1980

The Lure of Show Business

I loved New York and all of its marvelous diversity— being a biracial girl was not a problem in this multiracial and multicultural city. In New York I also learned that I loved—even more than the ballet—the world of commercial show business. I was a moth drawn to the proverbial flame of modeling and acting success. At first I thought I could do it all—be a model, an actress, *and* a ballerina. My mother was very disappointed that I wasn't going to focus solely on the ballet. I kept insisting to her that I wasn't leaving the ballet world. "I just want to branch out and model, act, and entertain." One of my mentors at the school, Stephanie

Saland, took my attraction to modeling and acting even harder than my mother. She came over one day and tried to make me understand what I was giving up. She was in tears. "You're so incredibly talented. You're about to be invited to join this company." To be invited to join the New York City Ballet Company was an incredible honor—not every student at the school would make it. But I still wanted it all.

What my mother and Stephanie understood, but I didn't at the time, was that the ballet does not allow such diversions. I had to choose. So I left the ballet. The transition was painful, but I had my heart set on modeling and show business. No one could change my mind.

My first break in modeling came about through a very famous fashion illustrator, Antonio Lopez. Jerry Hall, Jessica Lange, Tina Chow, Grace Jones, and Pat Cleveland had all worked with him. Lopez was often called "The Discoverer" of models. Among his clients were Valentino, Versace, Lagerfeld, Halston, and Issey Miyake. He did ad layouts for Bloomingdale's every week. Antonio was hot, and I knew it. I was twenty when I first met him through a fellow dancer who had a friend who had a roommate who knew Antonio.

Antonio was wonderful. He immediately made an appointment for me with the Eileen Ford Agency, and she signed me on the spot. He also set up a fashion shoot for me with one of the top brunette models at that time, Janice Dickinson, who was being photographed by one of New York's most successful fashion photographers, Mike Reinhardt.

I arrived at the shoot a total nervous wreck. As I was walking down a hallway in the studio I heard a woman screaming, "Is that Tatiana? Is that girl Tatiana? Is that her?" It was Janice Dickinson. At the time I was going by the stage name "Tiana." My real name is Stephanie Thumbtzen, but I had changed it to Tiana while living in New York. I thought "Tiana Thumbtzen" sounded so much more exotic. At least it seemed that way to a thirteen–year-old girl who dreamed of seeing her name on a marquee. In an instant, however, "Tiana" was lost to a new, even more exotic name given to me by one of the world's most successful fashion models. From that moment on I was Tatiana Thumbtzen.

When I met the woman who had just renamed me, I was overcome by her beauty. She was tall, slender, and really the most exotically gorgeous creature I'd ever seen. I just couldn't believe I was looking at the real Janice Dickinson. She came up to me and gave me a big hug and was very kind and friendly.

Taking a break from her shoot, Janice spent some time with me and gave me makeup tips and advice about entering the modeling business. I told her about my meeting with Eileen Ford, and she said Ford was the wrong agency for my type. I had a very exotic look. She advised me to seek representation from Elite or Zoli. "They will understand your type, your special look," she told me. "Ford is a mistake. She won't know what to do with you. You're not black enough or white enough." Once again I felt like the biracial kid from Clearwater. What was she saying to me? What did she mean?

Then Janice started talking about the problems she had when she was starting out. She explained that agents laughed at her and complained about her "big nigger lips." "Now they're the rage," she gloated. "They're paying me thousands for these big lips. Look who's laughing now." I hated to hear the word *nigger*, even if she was talking about what someone else had said. It was so insulting.

I didn't take her advice and stayed with Eileen Ford. But

at the end of the first week with the agency, one of the talent bookers told me that she had no idea how to sell me. "You're not black enough. You're not white enough. We don't know how to categorize you." Then she dumped me. "Stick with Antonio. He seems to be helping you, and you're better off with him." I was in shock. I thought about what Janice Dickinson had said only a week before—advice I had ignored, thinking that somehow I had risen above the limitations of coming from a mixed racial background. I had reasoned that my look wasn't about race—it was about humanity. Why should anyone care about my race? Once again I was the oddball, the different outsider.

Clearly my color-blindness was naive. I believed that modeling was about beauty, not about race, but I had a great deal to learn. Modeling is part of a business that sells products to people. Certain races buy certain products. It's not a color-blind world. That reality was hard to swallow.

I got on the phone to Antonio. I was sobbing so much that he could barely understand me. I told him that Eileen Ford had dropped me in just one week. "What am I going to do?" I cried. I was barely twenty years old, had done only one modeling job, and figured that my career was over. Jumping in the first cab I could hail, I headed for Antonio's.

He put his arms around me when I arrived. I was still shaking and crying. "Don't worry," he consoled me. "It often takes going through a few agencies until you find the right one. Don't take it personally. We'll find the right one for you." Antonio got on the phone with Zoli and scheduled an appointment for me the following day. From devastation, there was renewed hope. I got myself together and prepared to meet the new agents.

The next day I walked into Zoli's office and met with Zoli himself. He was a very hard, cold man. I couldn't figure out what he was thinking or feeling behind his eyes of steel. But he must have been feeling good enough to give me a break. The agency signed me on the spot, just like Ford had done the week prior. "Ford's loss is our gain," they told me.

More importantly, Zoli actually sent me out, and I began to get some bookings. Several months into our contract, Zoli introduced me to an agent named Satoru, from Japan. Before I knew it, I was off to the Far East on a one-year contract. In only my third job in the modeling business, I did the cover for a magazine called *More*, a kind of Japanese *Vogue*. I soon became one of the top models in Japan and the Orient for the next five years.

NEW YORK CITY AND LOS ANGELES, 1984

Tinseltown Beckons

Not long after beginning my modeling career, I made my first forays into the world of film. The first movie I did was *Beat Street*, co-produced by Harry Belafonte. The film starred Rae Dawn Chong and was a hot film when it was released in New York.

Belafonte was wonderful to work with. At one point he took me aside and gave me some fatherly advice. "You know, you must learn to work harder and be better than the next guy, because you stick out like a sore thumb. You're very beautiful, but you're different." Then he warned me, "Beware, because they will throw you if they can." I didn't know what he meant then, but years later I would certainly learn.

Beat Street led me to Hollywood. It was my first taste of "the business" and I felt the sky was the limit. My next job was a music video with Herbie Hancock called "Hardrock." It came right at the tail end of his successful video, "Rockit." The year was 1984. By 1986 I was living in Hollywood permanently.

Professionally I seemed to fit better in Tinseltown than I did in the Big Apple. My dance talents were in demand because music videos were on the rise. I met a lot of people, and with the help of my then-boyfriend who was also a dancer, I was called for audition after audition. Soon I was recruited by agent Nina Blanchard. With my dream held tightly in my fist, I vowed to follow Harry Belafonte's advice. I would work harder and be better than my competition to land the right roles to further my career.

LOS ANGELES, 1986

Billy Dee Williams Loses My Respect

One of the first jobs Nina booked for me opened my eyes to some of the obstacles I would face in pursuing my Hollywood dreams. It was a print modeling job for Billy Dee Williams Eyewear. When I showed up on the set, Billy Dee was there and he was in a pretty foul mood. Apparently he was angry about his wife or girlfriend. Even though it was only ten in the morning, I could smell alcohol on his breath. As the day wore on, he began to flirt with me. I tried to just laugh and brush him off.

On the last roll of film for the shoot, I was standing near him and was directed to sort of hover over him. He was seated behind a screen so you could only see him from the chest up. As the photographer started to shoot, I felt Billy Dee's hand touch my right thigh. I thought it was just an accident and didn't react. But then he suddenly grabbed my crotch and held on tight. A shocked expression flashed across my face as I let out a little scream and jumped back. Everyone on the set knew that something had happened. The photographer stopped and fortunately said that we were done. I quickly ran off the set without speaking to anyone.

At that point I had been around celebrities for many years of my life. I always had respect and admiration for their accomplishments. I had been an admirer of Billy Dee Williams's work in *Mahogany* and other films, but I lost all respect for him after that photo shoot. I was hurt, disappointed, and disgusted by his behavior.

I considered talking to my agent about what had happened, but in the end I didn't report the incident to anyone. Like so many other young models and actresses, I was afraid that my career would be hurt if I spoke out about sexual harassment.

This experience was about ten years ago, before the example of Anita Hill, but I don't think things have changed that much in Hollywood since then. Even today too many young women don't report or speak out about these kinds of experiences, fearing that their careers will be jeopardized. I didn't do anything then, but I'm telling the story now, in hopes that I can be one voice to help stop this all-too-common type of celebrity behavior.

HOLLYWOOD, 1987

A Turning Point—"The Michael Jackson Girl"

*I*n 1987 I signed with a new agency, Joseph, Heldfond and Rix, at the time a fairly powerful group. Julie, my agent, sent me on an audition for a Michael Jackson video, "The Way You Make Me Feel." I wasn't told, though, whose video this was for. But I discovered later that two hundred other hopeful young actresses tested for that part.

When they called me, I was told to walk and show some attitude. The scene took place on a street in a rough area. A bunch of guys start hassling the character I was reading for, taunting her with lines like, "Hey baby, what's up?"

Coincidentally, the very same thing had happened to me as I was on my way to the audition. Some guys had hassled me on the street, so you might say I was prepared. I ran through the scene a few times, and my audition was put on videotape.

A few days later I was summoned to a small dress rehearsal. It was the first time I learned that the video was with Michael Jackson. I was brought into a room by the video's choreographer, Vince Patterson. Michael was there but I was too shy to even look at him at first. Patterson directed me to go through some moves, which I followed perfectly. Finally I glanced up at Michael. He was sitting there in a red shirt, bopping to the music with this big, happy grin on his face. I saw him turn to the person next to him and say something. I later found out from David Banks, one of the video's writers, that Michael had said, "She's the one. The rest are extras."

I will never forget when my agent called to tell me that I had the job. I screamed so loud that all of Hollywood must have heard me. It was such a milestone accomplishment

199

for me. I felt like I had finally made it, and my career would soon be taking off.

The shoot lasted five days, with the fifth day devoted to outtakes and close-ups of me. By the second day the ice was broken between Michael and me. It happened in the middle of a scene where he was chasing me, and I was supposed to run through a broken-down, beat-up car in the middle of a street. My dress was so tight that in order to cross to the other side of the car to get out, I had to turn around. During one take, in the process of turning, my high-heeled boot got caught in the upholstery, and I couldn't get it out. Michael put his hand on my calf and then on my upper thigh to help pull me out. I got a little overheated, I guess, and lost it. I fell out of the car, landing on my butt. We both cracked up as he wiped my butt off. Then we looked into each other's eyes for a moment. After that a warm and friendly connection started to develop between the two of us.

As we waited around on the set in the days after that scene, Michael began asking me questions about my life. A few times he was a little flirtatious, like when he told me I had an incredible walk. I said, "Well, it's just a walk." He looked at me and smiled. "No, you have a very *sexy* walk."

Not long after the video production was over, Michael's stand-in, Craig, who had become a friend of mine, called and said, "You know, Michael talks about you all the time. He asks me how you are and told me to tell you hello. I think he really likes you. He says stuff like how incredibly beautiful you are and how sweet you are."

Craig suggested that I come by and visit the set of another video Michael was shooting. I thought it was a great idea, so Craig asked Michael, and a few days later I was invited to drop by the set. It was fun being there and seeing Michael again. He showed me around the set, then I watched the filming and had something to eat with him and his manager in his trailer. At the end of the day I realized I didn't have a ride home. Still a recent transplant from New York, I didn't drive yet. The cab to the studio had cost more than I had expected, and I didn't have enough cash for a cab home. Craig pushed me to ask Michael for a ride.

Too shy to go to Michael directly, I explained my situation to Miko Brando, Marlon Brando's son and Michael's right-hand man, and asked if he could lend me a few bucks or give me a ride. Miko offered to check it out with Michael but thought it would be no problem to give me a ride in the limo. A few minutes later I was on my way home, sitting next to Michael in his black stretch Mercedes, which Miko was driving. At first Michael seemed nervous and jittery like a kid. We talked a lot, mostly about our families. At one point we were sort of holding hands. When he dropped me off, I thanked him and said I hoped to see him again. He said, "Oh, you will."

Shortly after that I was hired to go on Michael's *Bad* Tour to perform the sketch from the video live in Kansas City and New York. If it worked out, there were to be more appearances in other cities on the tour. Naturally I was thrilled to be working with M.J. again.

We did the Kansas City shows and then arrived in New York where we had three dates at Madison Square Garden. I had an idea for the end of the performance that I thought would improve the piece. After Michael's hot, intense pursuit of the girl I played, all he did at the end was give me a hug. It was kind of a letdown for the audience. People would come up to me and say, "If Michael is so much in love with this girl, why does he just give her a hug at the end?"

I wanted to discuss this problem with Michael and ask him if it would be all right to give him a kiss instead of just the hug at the end. But during the busy tour I was not able to see him or speak to him except when we were actually onstage performing. So on the second night of the perform- ance, at the end of the hug, I reached up and gave him a little kiss on the cheek. The crowd went ballistic. Michael seemed surprised, but he smiled. Afterward nothing was said by any of his handlers except the usual "Great show."

The next day was the last day I was scheduled to per- form, and I called Michael's secretary to ask her if I could talk to him. She gave me his number but told me not to keep him on the phone for too long because he was very tired. I reached him and thanked him for giving me the op-

portunity to work with him. I also said that I hoped my little kiss did not throw him off.

Michael assured me that the kiss was okay. "Can I take it a step further tonight?" I asked him. "Yeah, that would be great." he said. I thanked him again and hung up.

I was very nervous that final night as I got onstage. I kept questioning whether or not I should really kiss him. I knew the crowd would love it. But I was also under the impression, both from my time with Michael and from what others in the production company had told me, that Michael had a crush on me. I had sensed it from our eye contact, from gestures, from hugs, from sweet little things he said or did.

We got to the end of the act, and I was standing in front of him. My hands were on his collar and I was looking right into his eyes. He had this very sexy look on his face. He bit his lip. I pulled myself forward, toward him, and he put both of his hands on my hips. We embraced, and then kissed each other full on the lips. The crowd freaked out. I pranced off the stage, and Michael went on singing and laughing, entertaining with more life in his voice than I had ever heard before.

When I got backstage, all of the dancers congratulated me on how great the show was and how happy Michael seemed to be. I loved the wonderful response to the show. But for me it was more than just a performance. I really liked him, and I knew that he liked me, too. I felt there was something there between us.

When we got back to the hotel, John Draper, the tour manager, came up to me, and I went with him to take care of my hotel bill. While we were standing at the registration desk, Miko Brando came out of nowhere and started screaming at me at the top of his lungs. "How fucking dare you do that to Michael?" he yelled. "You bitch, you fucking bitch, what were you doing? How can you take advantage of him like that in front of all of those people?'' He went on and on, obviously having no idea that Michael and I had talked beforehand. It seemed so off the wall.

Then Michael's manager, Frank Dileo, walked past. After every prior show, Frank would tap me on the shoulder and tell me how great I was. That night he didn't say a word but instead gave me the most evil look I have ever seen.

To this day I have no idea what I did that was so terrible, but that was the end of the tour for me. I was not asked back when the *Bad* tour went on to several cities. Sheryl Crow took my place.

I went home and cried incredibly hard—over both the lost opportunity and over losing Michael. His mother, Katherine, was also puzzled by what happened. She later invited me several times to the Jackson compound in Encino and we talked at length. She told me that when we were shooting the video, Michael had asked her what he should do with me. He had told her how much he liked me and that he had feelings for me. She had told him to express himself, to tell me about his feelings.

He never did tell me anything of the kind, although several others in his camp—bodyguards, secretaries, and writers—had let me know. The only explanation I could fathom was that Michael's top managers must have seen me as a threat. The *Bad* tour was one of the most successful promotions of his career, and the people working for him did not want anything to mess it up—especially a relationship with some girl they hardly knew.

Perhaps they thought of me as someone who, like a crazed fan, imagined herself being lovers with the superstar. Michael had done a music video of "Dirty Diana" with a similar storyline. To me, however, the feelings between us had always seemed very mutual. I felt a bond with him. Maybe it was because he, too, seemed to want to think of the world as color-blind.

Perhaps, however, I was naive or mistaken or read too much into some of the things that happened between Michael and me. Even if that is so, I always behaved in a completely professional manner. Unfortunately, being fired from that tour had terrible repercussions for me both psychologically and professionally. I hope I will be able to put the experience behind me someday and go on, but for years it has haunted me. Certainly it illustrates how show business, money, and greed can keep apart two people who care for each other.

ENCINO, 1989

Joseph Jackson Misquides My Career

After leaving the Michael Jackson tour, Joseph Jackson, Michael's father, wanted to sign me to a management contract. Like Michael's mother, he also sympathized with me and didn't like what had happened to me on the tour. When he proposed that he become my manager, I hoped he might really be able to help me. I had never had any problems getting contracts with agents or managers but finding one who could really build my career seemed to be the real challenge. I knew that Joseph was quite the ladies' man, but he never tried to have his way with me. At the time we met he had a little Asian girl under contract, to whom he paid a lot of attention—unfortunately more than he ended up paying to me professionally.

After a while I realized that Joseph wasn't going to be able to help me. In fact, I suspected that being under contract to him was probably hurting my career. All I wanted was to get out from under his control, but everyone to whom I showed the contract, including agents and lawyers, told me I was locked in. They said I needed a high-powered attorney with connections, but I had neither the money nor the clout to get one.

HOLLYWOOD, 1990

Looking for Help from a Friend—A Few Dates With De Niro

While still under contract with Joseph Jackson, I took a job as a coat checker at the China Club in Hollywood.

Many people who knew me felt that my career should have been taking off in light of the success of the Jackson video. Well, nothing was really taking off at that moment, and I needed to pay my bills. On one of my nights off, I got a call from the club manager, Danny. He asked me to come in the next day to meet someone, a friend of his named Bobby.

"Bobby wants to meet you," he told me. "He saw your picture in my office, and he thinks you're beautiful. It would be to your benefit to get in here tomorrow and meet him." Then his tone of voice changed. "Hey, I'm talking about Bobby De Niro, the greatest actor in the world, you know?" To Danny, this was a big career-making opportunity for me. "Maybe he could put you in one of his films or something like that."

I agreed to meet the great De Niro. Of course, I was also savvy enough to realize that this was Hollywood and that neither Danny nor De Niro was likely to have much interest in helping my career.

I arrived at the China Club the next night with my girl-friend Angela. My friend Antonio had warned me years before about De Niro. He had said to watch out for him—he's a "player"—so I didn't want to go on this venture alone. Danny saw me come in and said he had not seen De Niro yet that evening, so Angela and I sat and waited. A half an hour went by, and Danny came by again. I asked him what was up. "Is he coming or not?" Danny just shrugged his shoulders.

Then Angela said, "Isn't that De Niro over there?" Sure enough, he was sitting with another guy and a couple of women. "How strange," I thought to myself. "I'm asked to come here to meet De Niro for some kind of date, and he's sitting there with two other women."

I waited a few more minutes and the women at his table got up and left. Angela and I took our cue and went over to where he was sitting with his friend. I extended my hand

and said, "Hi, I'm Tatiana. It's nice to meet you." De Niro acted as though he had no idea who I was, as though I were some anonymous fan coming over to him. He also seemed to have no idea who Danny, the manager, was. I was totally stunned.

I turned to Angela, who whispered, "This is total bullshit. It's a bunch of crap." I agreed. De Niro and his friend invited us to sit down with them. We did and shot the breeze with the two men for a few minutes. Then De Niro said he and his friend had an appointment and had to leave, but he would call me later.

"You don't even have my number," I replied as he got up. He had a little smirk on his face, one that I'd often seen in his films. "Oh, don't worry," he said. "I've got your number." I thought he must have been kidding. Angela and I stayed a while and danced. By the time we left the club, I had put the entire thing out of my mind.

The phone rang less than fifteen minutes after I got home from the club. I was surprised when I heard De Niro's voice and had mixed feelings. On the one hand, I was honored that he called me. But I was also put off by his bravado and self-assurance. Yes, he was the great Robert De Niro, and it was nice that he found me intriguing enough to call, but why had he been so aloof at the club? It was also frightening to think that Danny was giving my number out without my permission—pimping me to his star patrons. It made me feel cheap.

I felt a little better after we talked a minute. De Niro was very sweet. "I wanted to call to see if you got in safely. Would you care to go out some time?" I said that would be nice. He told me he had to go to New York and would call me when he was back in L.A.

When he returned we made a lunch date. He picked me up at my modest little apartment. When he came in he immediately noticed an enormous portrait of me on my wall, done by Antonio in 1982. It was from a special piece that had been written about Antonio in *People* magazine, which had featured pictures of some of his models. My picture was shown, as was Toukie Smith's, another of Antonio's models and a longtime love interest of De Niro's.

He knew right away that the photo was Antonio's work. I hoped that he would say something about his relationship with Toukie, but he didn't. I wondered if their affair was over. I'm not the kind of woman who wants to be the other woman, causing the pain.

We went to a little industry place in Studio City called Residuals. He was worried that he would be recognized and bothered, but I assured him that it was just a quaint local hangout and that nobody would care. Sure enough, with the goofy-looking reading glasses he was wearing, not even the waitress recognized the great De Niro.

I did not think Bobby De Niro was a great conversationalist. At least he wasn't at the start of our date. He didn't act like the kind of man who is really interested in you. At first I got the impression that all he wanted to do was jump my bones. So I decided to keep the conversation on a professional level. I talked to him about my problems with Joseph Jackson, hoping that he might know someone who could help me get out of that contract.

Once I started talking about my career, he responded with a few questions about my life. At that point things seemed to change, and I began to feel that he might be genuinely interested in me. He looked right at me and seemed truly engaged in listening to my story. We finished our lunch, and he drove me home. There was no kiss, just a kind good-bye and a promise to meet again. It turned out to be a very nice first date.

On our second date we went to a Japanese restaurant

downtown and once more talked for hours. Again De Niro wanted to know all about me. At the end of the evening he took me home, dropped me off, and that was it. He was a total gentleman. He was so respectful that I thought he really liked me. After all, he spent time with me, listened to me, and seemed to care.

The next time Bobby called was one night when I was at home and my friend Connie was over. We were sitting around watching TV when the phone rang. He was in his bungalow at the Beverly Hills Hotel and wanted me to come over. "Just drop over for a while. We'll have a few drinks. Bring your friend if you want," he said. He reassured me that nothing was going to happen. He had a friend there, too.

It was rather late and Connie was suspicious. She didn't think we were going to be a foursome for bridge at midnight in a bungalow at the Beverly Hills Hotel. We decided to go, but the plan was that we would stick together. Soon after we arrived at the bungalow, however, De Niro's friend wanted Connie to drive him to a club to pick up his car. She didn't really want to leave me, but I reassured her that I would be fine.

After they left, Bobby gave me a Lite beer and sat down next to me. I brought up my Joseph Jackson contract again. "I don't want anything from you, but I could use your advice."

"Yeah, no problem," he replied. The last time I had seen Bobby, he had asked me to bring a copy of my contract the next time we saw each other. He now asked if I had it with me. I nodded and pulled the document out of my bag to show him.

He took it, looked it over a bit, and threw it on the couch. Then, all of a sudden, he turned into an octopus. His arms were everywhere. He was grabbing me, holding me, trying to kiss me. The more I pushed him off, the harder he tried to kiss me.

I went into what I call my New York mode. "Don't be so frickin' aggressive," I yelled. "You don't have to squeeze me to death!"

Then we locked lips. In the middle of this major kiss with De Niro, I again had mixed emotions. On the one hand, I thought, "Wow, I'm kissing De Niro." On the other hand, I felt he couldn't care less about me. The kiss wasn't loving and warm. I didn't find it sensual at all. He was aggressive and hard. My lips were locked to his as he held my body in a tight stranglehold.

I soon came to my better senses and again began to fight him off. I hit him and yelled, "You don't really care about me or my problem with Joseph Jackson's contract. My life is just a joke to you." As quickly as it all began, he suddenly released me, apologizing profusely. "I'm sorry. That's not true. I do care," he said, attempting to win back my affection.

I wasn't convinced, but he continued. "What you need is a good attorney to look at that contract. That's the bottom line." I thought to myself, "Duuuh, like I didn't know that."

Then he got up off the couch and excused himself. "Would you mind if I changed into something more comfortable?" he asked. I wondered, "Am I living in some old movie? Isn't the girl supposed to deliver that line?" Seconds later De Niro came out of the bungalow bedroom wearing nothing but a Beverly Hills Hotel thick white terrycloth bathrobe.

I couldn't believe the whole thing. I thought to myself, "He put his arms all over me, and now he's taken off his clothes and put on a robe. What am I supposed to think is going to happen next?" I wanted to leave.

He must have read my mind. "Come on, don't worry. I'm not going to do anything. Just come here for a second. I'm not going to hurt you or do anything," he said, pulling me into the bedroom. He was certainly convincing. I was still in my New York mode, however. "I know I'll be okay, because I'll kick your ass if you try anything." He laughed.

In the bedroom he suddenly opened his fancy robe. There he was, naked, flashing me. He hopped up on the bed and jumped up and down, giggling like a little boy. Actually it was funny. I just looked at him, thinking, "If only my friends could see me now. Here is Robert De Niro flashing me, dancing on the bed like a wild man!"

After that display, he then crawled under the covers. I guess he thought his antics were an enticement for me to join him. Wrong. "This is ridiculous," I said. "Please call me a cab."

"Okay, okay, I'll call you a cab. No problem, I'll call the cab," he said. Before he called the cab, however, he made one more attempt to get me into bed. He got out from under the covers, grabbed me, threw me down on the bed, and kissed me again. I pulled back, caught my breath, and said, "What would you do if there was a fire in this hotel right now?" God knows how I thought of that line. "Well, I guess I'd run out of here," he replied. "You'd run out of here if there was a fire?" I repeated. "Wow, then everyone would say, 'There goes De Niro, what a little weenie!'"

It was a poor choice of words, I'll admit. I didn't mean his private parts, which were okay sizewise. I just meant it as a joke about how he wouldn't be the tough guy he often plays in his films. The truth is, I was simply trying to distract him so I could get away. It worked. He called a cab and I left.

As I walked out of that bungalow I felt very disappointed by how he had handled himself. I wanted to believe that he liked me, but I was clearly naive to think that this man wanted me to come to his hotel suite in the middle of the night to talk about my career problems. All he ever wanted to do, like so many famous men in Hollywood, was to get me in bed. My first impression had been right. Even though I found him very attractive, I was not ready to sleep with him. He was still a stranger I hardly knew.

I'd heard the talk about De Niro, but if he had wined me, dined me, romanced me, and perhaps really helped me with my contract, it just might have worked. I might have been with him if he had convinced me that he cared about me. Instead, he made me feel like a piece of raw meat—or a trophy for his collection. I had too much self-respect to let anyone make me feel that way.

De Niro called me a couple of weeks later. I told him how I felt, and he apologized. He then asked me to go to the movies with him, and we went to see *Pretty Woman*. After the show I told him that perhaps the character played by Julia Roberts had found her prince, but I didn't think that I had found mine. I wished him well, good luck, and goodbye. He dropped me off. I got out of the car and never looked back.

HOLLYWOOD, 1990

Jerry Buss Tries to Make a Deal

Many women in this town have stories about the owner of the Los Angeles Lakers, Jerry Buss, and I'm no exception. I met Jerry through an actor who was a mutual friend. Jerry asked me out to dinner, and I accepted. As we were in his limousine, before we even had dinner, Jerry proposed a deal. He started with flattery. He said that I was incredibly beautiful. I was like a swan, like a gazelle. The way I held myself was so eloquent. Then he said, "I need a woman with your class by my side, on my arm." He offered to take care of me, to get me a car and a nice apartment, and to take care of my bills if I would perform the service of being at his side—and presumably whatever else that entailed.

As I listened to all of this, I almost choked on my champagne. Though God knows I could have used the car, the nice apartment, and the help with my bills, I knew his deal wasn't for me. I tried to be diplomatic with him—after all, I still had to sit through dinner—and told him I would think about it. He nodded, "Well, you think about it. You might need me someday."

At dinner, as I sat across from him, I tried to imagine myself ever being attracted to him. I just couldn't. He was simply a nice older man. I remembered, of course, that this was Tinseltown—a decadent place where older, rich men think they can buy anything they want, including women. What's sad is that a lot of women in this town do make these deals with men like Jerry Buss. Some become their mistresses, others may even get to be their wives. But they sell themselves short. They may get access to the material things, but they lose their soul.

I turned down Jerry Buss's offer, of course. But one thing I can say for Jerry is that despite my not taking him up on his proposition, he has always been warm and charming whenever I've run into him since that evening. He continued to invite me to Lakers games, and once he even gave me a print job on a shoot for a "Laker Girls" calendar. The money from the job didn't buy the car or the apartment, but it was honest work and it helped with a bill or two.

I Did Have a Prince in My Life

Though neither Robert De Niro nor Jerry Buss turned out to be my "prince," I did meet someone who was, for a time, a real Prince to me. I met the artist formerly known as Prince at a birthday party my friends threw for me at the West Hollywood Club 20–20. At one point during the party I was looking out the window and turned around to see Prince standing across the room. I was taken by how beautiful he is in person, even more so than on camera. Since it was my birthday, I walked over to him, introduced myself, and asked him to dance. He accepted, and we moved onto the dance floor. He spun me around, and soon everyone in the club seemed to stop and watch us. We danced for a while then talked and had a great time.

As the party wound down, he invited me to go for a ride in his limo. We rode around for a couple of hours, listening to demos of his new music. What a birthday. I felt like Cinderella.

Neither of us seemed to want the evening to end. He asked me to come to his hotel, and I agreed. I told him I was hungry, and he ordered tons of food, but he never touched any of it himself. At one point we were talking, sitting cross-legged on the floor. I mentioned that I was shy. Suddenly he reached over and pulled my top down for a second. I looked shocked and he said, "I thought you were shy!" Then, referring to my breasts, he said, "They're so beautiful! Do you ever hold them or play with them?" I looked at him like he was crazy and said, "No!" He laughed. "Why not? I would if they were mine."

Next he led me to his big walk-in closet. He had hundreds of suits in every color of the rainbow and boots to match. I was mesmerized. I tried on his boots, and they were a perfect fit. "Maybe I'll dress you up in my clothes some night," he said. I sort of nodded. The boots fit, but I estimated the pants would be too short since I was 5'7" and he was only 5'4".

It was now about four or five in the morning. He invited me to stay, promising to take me home in the morning. I felt so comfortable with him that I agreed. He gave me a pair of silk pajamas to change into, and he put on a black Lycra catsuit. We kissed and cuddled as we drifted off to sleep. It had been a magical evening.

After that first date, Prince and I went out a few more times. One evening he admired the belt buckle I was wearing. It was a big, bold silver buckle that spelled out "Love," a throwback to the Andy Warhol pop culture days of the 1960s, made famous once again by Madonna in the 1980s with her "Boy Toy" thing. I decided to get a similar belt buckle made for Prince. I called a friend in New York City and ordered one for Prince in gold that spelled out his birth sign, Gemini, something he had hinted that he would like.

The next time I saw Prince, he sent his brother, Dwain, in a Rolls-Royce to pick me up. I brought the belt buckle gift with me but left it in the back of the Rolls. I didn't want to give it to Prince directly, since I knew that he didn't like to be handed gifts. At my birthday party he had said, "Gifts, I don't like gifts." Dwain promised to give it to him later.

A few weeks later I was watching TV and saw Prince's

new video, "Batdance." I was impressed with his incredibly awesome work. At one point the theme of the video switched to astrological signs, and there was Prince wearing the belt buckle I had given him. I was very touched, to say the least.

During the next several months, Prince and I shared a few more romantic interludes. There were moments of passion, but he never went too far. Prince seemed to treasure me in some way. He placed me on a romantic pedestal. I felt like the doll of a child who cherished and protected his favorite toy.

The closeness we had, however, was more important than any sexual feelings. We talked and talked—there was nothing we didn't talk about. And we'd laugh together hysterically. I had a delightful time with him.

Prince is wonderful, but he is also eccentric. Along with his brilliance, there is a temperamental side—and I've seen both his Dr. Jekyll and his Mr. Hyde. His mood could change at the drop of a hat. He'd be fine one minute, then dark, dramatic, and withdrawn the next. I learned to go with the flow. It was the only thing to do.

Prince and I lost touch for about four years. We met by chance one night at a club and started talking about an interview I had given to the *Star* during the scandal involving Michael Jackson and the underage boy. Prince, who was upset with me for having spoken to a tabloid, attacked me for comments that were attributed to me in the piece. I did the interview to be supportive of Michael, but part of the article came out twisted and negative. Prince was bothered by a line that quoted me as saying that Michael would never get married. In truth, I never actually said that, but that didn't matter to Prince.

"Did you need the money that bad?" he asked me. "Are you that poor, that broke, that you have to sell your story to the tabloids?'' Actually, I had been having a very rough time financially, and the *Star* offered me five grand to tell the story of my experience with Michael. Unfortunately, the tabloid made my story sound very different from what I had really said. It was a learning experience for me, but Prince couldn't and wouldn't forgive me. I never saw him again after that. He was probably afraid that I would sell the story of our friendship one day. Well, here it is. This time, however, you're reading the simple truth, without distortion.

HOLLYWOOD, 1993

An Encounter with Bad Boy Bobby Brown

One night in 1993 my friend Iris Parker and I were going to the Roxbury, a club on West Hollywood's Sunset Strip. Iris used to sing with Madam X, and now she's doing backup vocals for former Supreme Mary Wilson.

As we waited in line on the VIP staircase, Bobby Brown and a group of his buds came up behind us. Right away he touched my butt. "So, how are you doing with your sweet ass?" he said. I turned around. "How could he be so crass," I thought. "Fine" is all I said.

He recognized me from my work with Michael Jackson and started talking to me about a video he was doing. He told me he wanted me to be in it. After we entered the club, and throughout the night, he kept talking to me about doing a video for him. He was living it up with the guys, but he kept coming over to talk to me. At one point he said, "I don't want none of that Michael Jackson shit, either."

He told me that he wanted me to do some hip-hop and a whole different style of dancing.

"I'm a dancer, I'm versatile," I told the self-assured, cocky Bobby Brown. "I do all types of dance. Just tell me what you want," I said.

At the end of the evening, while Iris and I were waiting for the valets to bring our car around, he came up to me and whispered in my ear, "You know, when I saw you in that video with Michael Jackson, all I wanted to do was to put a hole in you where there wasn't a hole before." I hauled off and whacked him on the arm. Iris and I wondered how such a low-life, classless guy could be married to Whitney Houston. At this time they had been married about four or five months, and she was already pregnant. Yet here he was, propositioning me. "You're a married man," I said to him. Without missing a beat he said, "Baby, this is all about business with me. It's money, that's it. I'm all about business."

He was drunk and rude. It seemed like ten minutes had passed, and our cars still had not come. Bobby Brown was still going on about "business." Naturally I realized that the video gig was just a carrot he was holding out to hook me. The real business was about sex, which was not any business I wanted. It was typical Hollywood bullshit business. I'd been offered that kind of a deal more than once before.

HOLLYWOOD, 1996

Lessons Learned in the Pursuit of a Hollywood Career

*I*n Tinseltown, people are often very superficial. They look at the outer shell and miss the inner person. If you're hot, if you're successful, everyone wants to be your friend. But when you have a bad break or are going through rough times, the phone doesn't ring.

I know. I've been in both places. After the Michael Jackson video, people recognized me wherever I went. To this day people on the street still say to me, "Are you the girl in that Michael Jackson video?" Though I received a lot of recognition, I didn't make much money. And in some ways that recognition typecast me and made me lose other jobs I might have gotten, because I was too recognizable as "the Michael Jackson girl." The fame and notoriety put me in the fast lane. Well-known and successful men began to ask me out. But they were surprised when they came by my humble apartment, surprised that I couldn't afford a better place in a better neighborhood.

Hollywood is a town based on image, a lot of hype, and false hope. So many people here are floating around, trying to hitch themselves to elusive dreams of fame and fortune. It is so easy to lose sight of what is real in your life, of what is really important. In many ways I think I'm too real for this town.

My family, my friends, and my spiritual beliefs have kept me grounded, no matter how high I was flying. I was always taught that everybody is human, and no one is God. I've met a lot of famous people in this town, but I never idolized anyone. I've come to realize that even more important to me now than having a career is having a family. I've focused so much on work thus far in my life, and now my biological clock is ticking. I would love to find the right man to share my life with, and I'd like very much to have children.

As far as my career goes, perhaps it's over. I don't know. I still have a few dreams left. I know I'm talented. I know that if I were given the right opportunity I'd be great. But I may be supremely naive at thirty-six—even though I look much younger—to keep trying. Yet who can say what tomorrow will bring?

Perhaps I've held myself back because I have not used men—or let them use me—in order to get ahead. Certainly I've had my chances. But after turning down the likes of Robert De Niro, Jerry Buss, and Bobby Brown, I'm not going to start selling myself now.

To a very real degree in this industry and this town, women are still just objects in a male-dominated system. That's not to say that some women don't take advantage of the situation and use their bodies to fulfill their dreams. But I have never traded sex for work, money, or drugs. I have, however, sold my soul for the dream of fame, and I am paying the price for that every day of my life.

As Harry Belafonte told me at a very young age, "You'll have to work harder than anyone in order to make it. . . . They'll throw you if they can." I wasn't sure then what he meant. Now I know how right he truly was.

Jennifer

HEIGHT:	*5'7"*
HAIR:	*Blond*
EYES:	*Green*
WEIGHT:	*115*
PROFESSION:	*Singer/actress*
BORN:	*Los Angeles, California*
HOBBIES:	*Writing, horseback riding, and water sports*
EDUCATION:	*Beverly Hills High School; 1½ years of community college*
FIRST SEXUAL EXPERIENCE:	*At sixteen with a high school boyfriend*
GOALS AND DESIRES:	*To have a successful singing and acting career*
SEXUAL FANTASY:	*Making love on a tropical island beach as the warm waves crash over my naked body*
DRUGS:	*My drug days are over*
HAPPIEST MEMORY:	*First time singing live on the Joan Rivers show*
WORST EXPERIENCE:	*Hearing about my father's death*
DEALS/DATES/ ENCOUNTERS:	*Grant Show, Rob Camilletti, Nicolas Cage, Julian Lennon, Michael Landon, Jr., John Clark Gable, Heidi Fleiss, Nicollette Sheridan, Sylvester Stallone, Tatum O'Neal*

Growing Up in Beverly Hills

I'm afraid that many people from around the country—people who watch shows like *Lifestyles of the Rich and Famous*—believe that if you are the child of a famous celebrity or have grown up in Beverly Hills, your life is always wonderful, star-studded, and glamorous. Well, as my own story proves, the truth of the matter is that life is often no picnic in the Beverly Hills park.

First of all, the divorce rate in Beverly Hills has got to be one of the highest anywhere. When I was growing up, many of my friends' parents were divorcing. I can't remember any of those divorces being very amicable or even civilized. We witnessed plenty of flying dishes and even more flying words.

My family was no exception. My father was Gig Young, an Academy Award–winning actor whose career spanned three decades—from the forties to the seventies. He was in over sixty-five films, including classics like the original *Three Musketeers*, *Young at Heart* (with Frank Sinatra), *The Music Man*, and *Kid Galahad* (with Elvis Presley). He was nominated for a Best Supporting Actor Oscar three times and finally won in 1969 for *They Shoot Horses, Don't They?*

In the late fifties and early sixties, my dad was married to actress Elizabeth Montgomery. Their marriage lasted four years before they separated. During their separation he happened to look at a house for sale in Beverly Hills. The real estate agent who showed him the property was my mother. They fell in love. Dad divorced Elizabeth Montgomery, and my parents were married. A year later I was born.

My father was an alcoholic, but for the first year of his marriage to my mother he was sober—she convinced him to go to AA. For people addicted to alcohol or drugs, however, Hollywood is not an easy town to live in. My parents would often go out to dinner with Dad's show business friends, and his buddies would encourage him: "Gig, have a drink and loosen up. You're no fun sober." Soon he fell off the wagon, and my parents' marriage started to falter. Dad was paranoid when he was drunk, and he accused my mom of running around on him. He even tapped her phone. My mom, of course, became more and more unhappy with his drinking as time went on.

One night when I was one and a half years old, my father went too far. In a drunken rage he slapped my mother hard across the face. In the struggle, I ended up falling

down a flight of stairs. After that night my mother packed our bags, and the two of us left my father. He warned her at the time that if she left, he would never see me again. He knew how much my mother loved me and hoped that threatening to abandon me would convince her to stay with him. But even that cruel threat couldn't keep my mother in the unhappy marriage. My father kept his promise. I never saw him again after that night—except, like everyone else, in the movies and on television.

My Mother Became the Biggest Name in Celebrity Real Estate

After Dad was out of our lives, my mother, Elaine Young, had to become both mother and father to me. She didn't take anything from my dad and worked hard to build her own career. At first she worked for Mike Silverman, who in the 1970s was one of the biggest names in Beverly Hills real estate. Mike was Cary Grant–handsome, and a bachelor who played hard and sold hard. He also could be hard on those who worked for him. My mom would come home from work crying just about every day.

One day when I was still a little kid, I was at my mother's office. I walked up to Mike Silverman and asked, "Why do you make my mommy cry?" He never really answered but, in retrospect, I think he was jealous of her. She was starting to build her own reputation and was stealing some of his thunder.

It might have started when *60 Minutes* came to Beverly Hills to do a piece on Silverman, the "Realtor to the Stars."

During the taping my mother was in the background along with some of the other women in Silverman's office. When Mike Wallace fired his first question, Silverman, who didn't have the greatest answer, deferred to my mother. She answered it in a fun, direct, matter-of-fact way. Plus, she was beautiful. From that point forward, the cameras and questions were directed at her. That incident fueled the rivalry between my mother and Mike Silverman. Not long after that, she broke away from him and eventually formed her own company.

While my mother was building her career, she was also looking for the perfect man—and not always finding him. After my father she married a succession of husbands, in marriages that each seemed to last an average of four years. First there was Stanley Styne, son of Jule Styne, the famous composer/songwriter and co-writer of *Funny Girl*. After Stanley there was Sal Vilacchi, an Italian mobster-type from Chicago and actually the one I liked the most. Her next husband was a guy I couldn't stand at all, Jonathan. He borrowed money from my mother and got her involved in a company that failed, almost bankrupting her.

The stepfather with whom I had the most problems, however, was Bill Levey. When my mother married Bill Levey, our home turned into a battlefield. I was going through a rebellious stage then so I know I was part of the problem. They argued constantly over how to discipline me. He was a film director, known for directing Dorothy Stratten in her first movie, *Skatetown, U.S.A.* He had also cast Debra Winger in *Slumber Party '57*, her first movie. And, before I moved out of the house, Bill put me in my first movie. It was a bit part in *Lightning, the White Stallion* starring Mickey Rooney.

NEW YORK CITY AND BEVERLY HILLS, 1978

The Game of Death

*M*y father also remarried—and continued to drink. I would hear about him and see his movies, but he never broke down and visited me.

Gig Young met his last wife on the set of a film he was doing with Bruce Lee. The film's name, *The Game of Death*, seemed to be an ominous portent of things to come. First, Bruce Lee died during the filming. Then my father's new marriage turned volatile and violent. In angry moments his wife would taunt him and tell him that his career was over or that he was no good in bed. He was drinking more and more, and their fights kept escalating. One night, during one of their fights, he killed her. No one knows for sure how it happened, but I believe it was an accident. He must have had the gun in his hand and was trembling and shaking so hard that the trigger went off. He then turned the gun on himself. He obviously couldn't deal with what he had done and with the prospect of spending the rest of his life in jail.

I was fourteen years old when my father killed himself. After school that day, I opened the door to my house to find paparazzi flashing cameras in my face. I didn't know what was going on. I called my mother and she told me that my father had died. That night news of his suicide was on television and on the radio every hour. My mother was devastated. It was months before she was able to function normally. I cried a lot during that first night about this man I hardly knew, my father. It was really difficult for the reality to sink in. To this day it's hard to believe that my father killed someone else and then himself. It's almost impossible to fathom.

My mother sent me to a therapist after she and my father split. All those years of therapy helped me to survive everything that happened when I was a child. Even more important for my survival, however, was my mother's unconditional love. I always knew that she loved me and would be there for me, no matter what.

My mother and my therapist helped me to realize that, despite his behavior, my father also loved me. I don't feel anger toward him today because I know in my heart that his alcoholism robbed him of his family, his career, and ultimately his life. Alcoholism is a disease, and this disease killed my father, not the gun that actually took his life.

Although I don't feel anger toward my father any more, I am filled with sadness. I feel so sad about how he died, and I wish so much that he were here today. I still carry around a copy of his driver's license in my wallet. It's with me always and everywhere. I'd give anything to see him again, to run up and put my arms around him and tell him that everything is just fine and there are no hard feelings. I would give anything for ten minutes with him to tell him how much I love him.

BEVERLY HILLS, EARLY 1980S

Fast Times at Beverly Hills High

Like many other "celebrity kids," I went to school at Beverly Hills High. In the early 1980s when I was there, drugs were plentiful, nose jobs were incredibly popular, and there were parties all the time. Quaaludes, pot, and the legal standbys, tobacco and alcohol, were the drugs of choice. Kids often stepped off campus for a few minutes in between classes to get high. I was no exception. Once, right before an important spelling test that would make a difference in my grade, I left the campus with some friends and got stoned. It was a stupid thing to do. Miraculously, I managed a B-plus on the test.

My focus wasn't on learning. It was on parties and boys. In fact, I was an entrepreneur for a while when it came to parties. With a partner, a guy named David who died of a drug overdose after we graduated, I would throw huge parties in four and five million dollar homes and charge at the door. Both alcohol and drugs flowed freely at these parties, and to this day I don't know how the hell we got away with it. Sometimes the crowds would get rough, too. One time a fight broke out, and a guy went flying through a huge glass door out onto the street.

Another time, at a big house on Rodeo Drive in the "flats" of Beverly Hills, kids were drinking and throwing each other naked into the pool. All of a sudden an ambulance arrived. I ran to see who they had come for and was shocked to find out that one of my best friends from elementary school had overdosed. I thought she was going to die. Fortunately she didn't. The experience scared me enough to make me cool it for maybe a week or two, but then I was right back into the party scene again.

In a lot of ways I was just a normal teenager who was living in an abnormal town. I was not too interested in school, but was very interested in cute boys. I was a Beverly Hills brat living in the moment, totally involved with my friends and boyfriends, who were often other sons or daughters of stage, screen, or TV stars. Or they were on their own path to being part of the next generation of stars.

BEVERLY HILLS, EARLY 1980S AND
LOS ANGELES, 1987

A Sexy High School Nerd—Nicolas Cage

Nicolas Cage is a hot, Oscar-winning actor now, but back in high school he was a nerd, which is probably no surprise to his fans. It's easy to see that part of his personality. Nicolas was pretty crazy about me at Beverly Hills High, but my heart was somewhere else then. I would hang out with him and thought he was kind of attractive, but my main love was this guy named Mark Ezralow. Nick kept asking me out over and over again, and I kept turning him down. He never seemed to get the message that I was in love with Mark. I guess it makes sense that Nick Cage is so successful now—he knew at an early age never to take no for an answer.

Nick had a kind of superior attitude in school, or maybe it was a positive attitude. He'd walk around all day telling kids at school, "My uncle is Francis Ford Coppola, and I'm going to be a star." He used to say it way too much. Out of exasperation I'd say back to him, "So what? My father was an Oscar-winning actor . . . so there." We'd go round and round over such nonsense. Though it seems so infantile and silly now, then it was serious stuff. Those of us who were celebrity kids at Beverly Hills High measured ourselves and competed through our family résumés in show business.

I guess Nick Cage finally got the message about me when he asked me to the prom. I turned him down firmly. "Nicolas, I've got a boyfriend. I like somebody else. Actually I'm crazy about him, okay? Nothing personal or anything, but I'm seeing somebody else. End of story."

Well, it wasn't exactly the end of the story. Five years later I was having a little midnight snack with a girlfriend at Canter's Deli on Fairfax. Canter's is an "only in L.A." kind of place where hip Generation Xers mingle with little old Jewish ladies sipping late-night chicken soup. My friend and I were sitting in a booth gossiping and people-watching.

The next thing I knew, Nick Cage walked in and headed straight over to my booth. He had just finished doing *Moonstruck* with Cher, and was a hot young actor on the rise. I thought to myself, "Good for him. He's made it, just like he promised he would so many times in high school."

Suddenly there he was, pulling up a chair—not even asking the people at the next table if he could use it—and sitting down and looking at me. After staring at me for a moment he said loudly, "You never gave me the time of day in high school! You never gave a shit about me. You never would go out with me. You only cared about your redheaded boyfriend and his BMW. My little Pontiac Fiero wasn't good enough for you."

Canter's Deli is pretty packed on any given midnight. All the kids and the little old people there that night turned to look at us. My girlfriend, her mouth open, stared in disbelief at the spectacle. But Nick didn't stop. He went on for about ten minutes before I finally responded, "Yeah, you were really great in *Moonstruck*."

Then, all of a sudden, with the same intensity of his arrival, he departed. He put the chair back at the other table, thanked the people sitting there for its use, and left to join a table of five or six guys in another part of the restaurant. A few minutes later I was ready to go, and my friend and I headed for the cashier to pay our check. Everybody there was still looking at me. Nick saw us leaving and came over to me once more.

"Oh, no," I said. "You're not going to yell at me again about high school, are you?" To which Nick "Never-Take-

No-for-an-Answer" Cage replied, "Can I have your phone number?" I gave him my number, thinking that he probably thought I was giving it to him now only because he was a star. The truth was, I always had liked him, but in high school I was spoken for.

Nick did call me. It was around Thanksgiving, and he was going on a motorcycle trip north along the Pacific Coast Highway for a little turkey at his Uncle Francis Ford Coppola's Sonoma ranch. Part of me wished that he would invite me to ride on the back of his cycle, but then again, riding all night on the back of a motorcycle, even if it was with Nick Cage, was not my idea of a good time. Plus, I was seeing someone else now. We must have talked on the phone for a good hour before he left to go north.

STUDIO CITY, 1987

Kenny Rogers, Jr.—More Bad Timing for Nick Cage

I never heard from my jilted high school "wanna-be" lover Nick Cage again. He just had rotten timing with me. First, it was my high school boyfriend. Then, when he called after our Canter's encounter, I was seeing a very sweet man named Kenny Rogers, Jr., who I was crazy about. I thought he was adorable. At the time I ran into Nick Cage, I had been seeing Kenny for a couple of months.

After a date, Kenny and I would usually go back to his house in the Valley. His place was pretty ordinary—that is, ordinary for a guy whose dad was such a big and rich star.

The furniture looked like it all came from a beach house secondhand, and that's exactly where it did come from. Kenny Rogers Senior passed on to Junior his used beach-house furniture rather than discarding it or giving it away. Kenny shared with me that he and his dad were not very close, but that's about all he shared with me. We went out for some time, but we never went to bed together. I think that he was just very shy. After a while Kenny and I just "faded out"—that's movie talk for a short-lived relationship that went nowhere.

BEVERLY HILLS, EARLY 1980S

The Celebrity Kid Circuit—A Crush on Michael Landon, Jr.

Michael Landon, Jr., was another celebrity offspring who went to Beverly Hills High, and I had a major crush on him. Most of the time when we were in school we were both going out with other people, but when it was time for our senior prom there was a window of opportunity. My boyfriend, Mark, was a year older and didn't want to go to the prom with me. He thought it was "uncool" to go back to a prom once you had graduated. So I decided to ask Michael.

The timing was great because Michael had just broken up with a girl he had been seeing for a long time. Everyone in school knew what was going on—these breakups were always big news on campus.

I drove up to Michael Landon's huge house off Benedict

Canyon in Beverly Hills. I was really nervous as I walked to the door. One of the servants answered and ushered me into the house. I met Michael's mother, Lynn, who directed me up an enormous flight of stairs to his room.

"Hi," I said when I entered. He returned the salutation, knowing full well why I had come to his house. Like I said, everyone in all of Beverly Hills High knew that I was going to ask Michael to the prom. So I asked him, and he said yes. Utterly relieved, I quickly left.

When prom night arrived, Michael, looking great, picked me up in a limo. We danced until midnight and had a lot of fun. Then we went back to the guesthouse on his estate and fooled around until four in the morning. It was heavy petting, but we never went to bed together. The limo was long gone, so Michael had to take me home. We saw each other for the next couple of months but, as with Kenny Rogers, Jr., the relationship never went anywhere.

Michael later got married. I cried a little at the time because I always had a crush on him, even after we stopped seeing each other. But there was just too much pressure, too much each of us had to prove because of who we were and where we came from. It's too bad. When you're a kid you don't understand how little all of that really means.

BEVERLY HILLS, EARLY 1980S

Sharing Intimate Secrets with Nicollette Sheridan

Nicollette Sheridan and I were pretty much inseparable for a good couple of years during high school. She went to a private school, the Buckley School in Sherman

Oaks, but became part of our Beverly Hills High clique through Danielle and Carrie Earl, whose mother was married to Lee Iacocca. Nicollette and I had a couple of important things in common then. First, my high school boyfriend, Mark, was best pals with her long-term high school beau, a guy named Dominic. Second, we both loved to shop and could spend hours together at the malls. Like sisters, we would often buy the same outfit in different colors and then go out together wearing almost identical clothing.

Nicollette was a real girlfriend kind of girlfriend. We'd do our makeup together. We'd have slumber parties at each other's houses, the kind where you stay up all night revealing your deepest and darkest boyfriend stories to one another. She was a great friend.

People said that I was pretty hot in high school, but Nicollette was absolutely breathtaking. Everywhere we went we would get approached by guys and asked to be in some movie or to pose for some poster. Nicollette would literally tell them all to fuck off. She was smart—smarter than a lot of girls in Beverly Hills—and she knew that most of the men approaching us were not legit. I always thought, "Hey, this one might be for real," but she was just never interested. She thought it was all bull and would walk around with this "I'm not interested in your shit, leave me alone" kind of attitude. She was both smart and beautiful, in a town where many people have one of those assets but often not the other. She had both and she knew it.

Nicollette's life was no picture of normalcy, either. Her mother was also stunningly beautiful and always had really young boyfriends around, guys who were not much older than Nicollette. It was no big deal for these guys to spend the night with her mom. The next morning both

Mom and Nicollette would be walking around the house with practically nothing on. Nicollette would start bickering with her mother about something, and the guy would be standing there staring at the practically naked mother and her practically naked daughter going at it in the hall. It was always a circus at her house.

There was one night at Nicollette's house that I will never forget. We were sitting on the bed in her room sharing our most intimate secrets. I was wearing a skimpy T-shirt and bikini-type panties and so was she. We were laughing and giggling and telling boyfriend stories.

Dominic had been her boyfriend for years, but just recently Nicollette had met Leif Garrett, a teen singer and idol at the time. He was another member of our little clique of friends who hung out together. Nicollette told me that she was falling in love with Leif. "God, he's so great in bed," she said, going on and on about what a great a lover Leif was. I then shared some very intimate details about my boyfriend, Mark.

All of a sudden, Dominic popped out from underneath the bed. He started crying and yelled at Nicollette, "I just can't fucking believe you!" Nicollette freaked out, screaming back at him in the English accent she slipped into whenever she was really angry, "I cannot believe that you were hiding under my bed!" There I was, sitting there half-naked, having just told my personal best, witnessing this shouting match. All I could think of was that my life at school was over. My secrets would be all over town. Dominic would tell Mark every word I had said. Indeed, it was a tough few weeks after that. Nicollette's and my intimate secrets were the hot gossip of the moment. And Mark and Leif and Dominic all had it out over us.

Not long after that episode, Nicollette began to get serious about something else besides boys—her career. She realized that she was hot and turned her attention to acting. Looking back, I wish I had followed her lead and gotten as serious about my career at that young age. But I still had too much partying to do. After Nicollette's first movie, *The Sure Thing*, put her name and face out there, our friendship began to fade. I'm not the type of person to leave my friends behind, so it hurt my feelings. But hey, I've learned, more often than not, that's how it is in Hollywood.

MALIBU AND HOLLYWOOD, 1980S

More Celebrity Kids—Trouble with Tatum and Griffin O'Neal

Another celebrity kid I grew up with was Tatum O'Neal. She didn't go to Beverly Hills High, but I met her through one of my best friends, Andrea Feldstein. Leif Garrett, Nicollette Sheridan, and others in our little clique of friends all hung out a lot at Ryan O'Neal and Farrah Fawcett's beach house in Malibu. It was a spectacular place and I thought it was very cool to be out there. Tatum was another one of those Hollywood résumé kids. Her attitude conveyed, "Hi, I was the nine-year-old actress who won an Oscar." She thought she was simply ultracool.

Griffin was a troublemaker who would constantly do things just to annoy his father. One day when we were all at their beach house, Ryan got so angry at Griffin that he picked him up by the hand and leg and threw him into the wall. Leif and I and another friend watched in total shock. Despite the fact that Griffin was our friend, we sympathized with Ryan because Griffin was so bad all the time. We figured Ryan just lost it at that moment.

Like many of my friends from high school, Tatum and I stayed in touch for the next few years after we graduated. At one point, Tatum shared an apartment with Victoria Sellers, Peter Sellers's daughter. They lived in a cute place on Keith Avenue in West Hollywood and decided to have a little get-together for a close-knit group of twenty or thirty friends, including me.

The night of the party, their place was beautifully decorated. Candles were lit everywhere. Champagne was on ice, and the buffet spread was unbelievable—with great hors d'oeuvres, gourmet cheeses, you name it. The guests arrived, and everybody began partying and having a great time. I was hanging out with Tatum when out of nowhere she said to me, "Why don't you stay the night?" At first I thought it was just an innocent girlfriend thing—you know, spend the night, we'll have some more champagne, hang out, talk.

I didn't really feel like it but she persisted. "Why not? Why don't you spend the night?" she said. I started to think that maybe she had more in mind than talking. I told her that I didn't live that far away and was okay to drive home. Still, she wouldn't let up. I'd go off to talk with some other people in another part of the house, and she would follow me and ask again if I would spend the night with her.

Finally I figured I needed a phony excuse to get myself off the hook. "I've got to catch a flight to New York, and I've got to go home and get ready to leave in the morning," I lied. "No problem," she said. "I'll get you to the airport and take care of your car for you while you're gone."

I began to feel more and more uncomfortable. All I could think of was getting out of that house, even though I wanted to stay and party with my other friends. Finally I told Tatum that I had to go, and I'd call her when I got back from New York.

I could tell Tatum knew I was just trying to get out of spending the night. She walked me to my car and kissed me good-bye. It was just a quick kiss good-bye, but it was on the lips, which made me even more uncomfortable. I couldn't wait to get the hell out of there. I was so angry over the whole scene. I'm sure she knew from our mutual friends that I never went to New York at that time. Eventually, however, she got her revenge for my rejection of her proposition—she started going after guys she knew I liked.

MALIBU, 1987

Tatum Steals One of the Babys

I had a really big crush on John Waite, the former lead singer for a rock group called the Babys and writer of the 1984 hit song "Missing You." A friend of mine, Mario, knew John, and we all started hanging out together. One night a group of friends, including Tatum and me, were going to the Universal Amphitheater to hear John's solo concert. We all met at his hotel room, where he gave me some tennis shoes from Nike, the show's sponsor. I was having a great time. In all the excitement, however, I drank too much champagne and started to feel lousy toward the end of the show. After the concert, when we were all in John's limo on our way to hang out at Mario's beach house, I noticed that Tatum was flirting with John. When we got to his place, everybody was getting high, doing coke, and smoking pot. Everybody but me, that is—I was huddled in the bathroom, still sick from the champagne.

I finally decided that I was too sick to stay. I went home and left John in Tatum's clutches. The limo took me back to Coldwater Canyon, and Tatum took John to bed. She ended up hanging out with him and Mario at the beach for the next two days. She had her fun, but I have a feeling that it was less about John and more about getting back at me. She knew that I really liked him, and she wanted to give me a friendly reminder that you don't mess with the former nine-year-old Oscar-winning actress. Tatum, of course, went on to marry (and divorce) John McEnroe. And no matter how angry I have been with her at times, I was still sad when I heard that she had a problem with heroin. After all, I know from my own experiences that it isn't easy in this town. Who said a Hollywood childhood was such a gift?

HOLLYWOOD, 1986

The Celebrity-Daughter Game, with Jane Fonda and Katie Wagner

Another one of my childhood friends was Katie Wagner, daughter of actor Robert Wagner. We also hung out in the same circle of friends after high school. One night the two of us were out at Helena's, a hot club co-owned by Jack Nicholson. The club was packed with stars. George Michael was there. Jack Nicholson was at another table, and Katie and I ran into Jane Fonda in the ladies' room.

Katie was peeved at me that night because I had been dating a guy, Steve Jones, from the Sex Pistols, who she also liked. I wasn't seeing him anymore, but she was still holding a grudge about it.

Katie apparently decided to get even with me by schmoozing with Jane Fonda in the ladies' room and ignoring me. She walked up to Jane and said, "Hi, Jane. I'm Robert Wagner's daughter, Katie, and I just wanted to say hello."

Fonda replied, "Oh really? It's very nice to meet you." She glanced over at me as if to say, "And who's your nobody friend?" So I thought to myself, "Screw this. Watch me play the celebrity-daughter game." I smiled at the older-generation celebrity daughter Jane Fonda and said, "Hi, Jane. My name is Jennifer Young. My father was Gig Young."

She went crazy. Her entire attitude changed from cold and standoffish to practically drooling. "Oh my goodness, oh my God," she said, almost pushing Katie Wagner aside. "Your father was such a wonderful actor. I loved working with him in *They Shoot Horses*." She couldn't say enough about my father. Finally she took my hand and told me how good it was to meet me. Katie, meanwhile, had wandered over to a mirror to put on some lipstick and then disappeared out of the ladies' room. She was livid.

I think I always had felt a little inferior around Katie until that moment in the ladies' room with Jane Fonda. There is a kind of pecking order in the Beverly Hills celebrity-kids circuit, and I had felt that, after all, Katie's dad was alive and mine was dead. But that night in the trendy bathroom of that hip Hollywood club, my stock went way up, thanks to Jane Fonda, one of the biggest celebrity daughters of them all.

BEVERLY HILLS AND MALIBU, 1990

Second Generation Rogue—My Fling with Clark Gable's Son

John Clark Gable was another of my high school acquaintances who turned up later in my life. His mother was Kay Spreckels Gable, and his dad was the great Clark Gable. When I first met John I was dating another high school boy—not Mark, but probably the most popular guy in Beverly Hills High, Brent Weinberg, the son of producer Henry Weinberg.

Brent didn't need star credentials. He was absolutely gorgeous, and every girl in Beverly Hills wanted him. At least that's how it seemed to me. One day Brent and I were at the beach in Santa Monica and John Clark Gable walked over. Brent went into the water, and John asked me for my phone number. John was cute, but nobody could top Brent. I just smiled and walked away. John ended up getting involved with one of my best friends, Tracy. Brent and I eventually broke up, and I started dating Mark. While we were still in school, however, Brent was killed in a car accident. It was devastating to all of us who knew him. There must have been fifteen hundred kids at his funeral.

After we graduated from high school Tracy was still seeing John, and she would tell me all sorts of wild stories about him. I really didn't believe all of it, but I would find out for myself soon enough.

One night my mother was having a party at our house on Coldwater Canyon Drive, and Tracy and I were there. Tracy decided she wanted to fix me up with a friend of John's named Attila, a top model with that long, Fabio kind of hair and looks. I'd seen him around so I was game. She called John to get Attila's number and handed me the phone to say hello. John started in, "So how do you look now? You were so hot in high school. I always had such a crush on you. I always wanted you so bad. I don't want to set you up with Attila. I want to be with you myself."

Tracy was sitting next to me thinking that John was giving me his friend's phone number. I was thinking, "Well, Tracy's also seeing another guy. Maybe she won't mind. Then I can find out for myself if Tracy's stories about John are for real." I later asked her if she minded if I went out with John, and she didn't. I called John. We went on a couple of dates in town, and then he invited me to his beautiful home in Malibu. I was really nervous the first weekend I went out to his ranch, and I asked my roommate at the time to come with me.

John's place was really wonderful. There was a man-made pond in front of the house. Inside, right in the middle of the massive living room, was a Jacuzzi. Memorabilia of Clark Gable was everywhere, including a picture of the acting legend drawn by Walt Disney himself. John had a guest room for my roommate, and he treated her like royalty.

Even though this was my first time at John's Malibu home, it wasn't our first time together sexually. That happened a few weeks earlier. The experience had been indescribable. John completely rocked my world with his body. For those movie fans who wondered what Rhett did to Scarlett after he carried her up that sweeping staircase, if it was anything like what his son did to me, she was in heaven.

That night the three of us went to a bar in Malibu and hung out for a while, then returned to John's ranch. After my roommate went to her room, I joined John in his bedroom. That's where I learned firsthand about one of the strange things I'd heard from Tracy and never quite believed.

John Clark Gable wanted to make love to my feet! He had a foot fetish and wanted to fuck my toes. "How the hell are you going to do that?" I asked, in a state of amazement. First he painted my toenails. Then he put his penis between my big toe and second toe, and he fucked my foot, getting off by rubbing his penis back and forth between my toes!

"Jesus Christ, you like being with my foot better than you like being with me. This is unbelievable," I said to him. Fortunately he was with me as well—it wasn't *all* just penis-and-foot love. He definitely had a foot thing, though. He wanted foot love all the time during those few months. One month we went down to a private beach, open only to residents with keys to the gate. We were fooling around, kissing on the sand, and John said to me that he wanted to have sex.

"Okay," I said. "But what if someone comes?" No one was in sight, and John assured me that we would be alone. The next thing I know he wants to do the foot thing. He has my leg up in the air and his penis stuck between my toes and he's going for it full speed ahead. I started pleading with him to stop, fearing that someone would come along and see us doing this weird thing. Sure enough, a couple suddenly appeared from out of nowhere. John yanked his penis out of my toes, dove on top of me, and covered us with a blanket.

John apologized for that fiasco, and we continued to go out. Another weekend I was in Malibu, and John offered to install blinds on his master bedroom windows so that the morning sun wouldn't awaken me. This may seem like no big deal, but to John, offering to put blinds on those windows for me meant commitment. He was getting serious. I was ambivalent, however. I was really bored with him making love to my feet, though the rest of the sex was very good.

I invited John to dinner with my mother to see what kind of a person he was in that type of situation. He was very set in his ways for a young man, never having had to work a day in his life. He promised me that he would be on his best behavior to impress my mother—and he was. But that night I realized that being with John was just not right for me. I knew that I had to get out of the relationship. John must have called me thirty times a day for weeks after that dinner with my mother, but I never called him back. I didn't want to see him again. My feet had had enough. It was another celebrity-kid union that just, well, got off on the wrong foot.

BEVERLY HILLS, 1985

The "Older Men" Circuit Leads Me to Julian Lennon

As angry "first wives" know, it is a common phenomenon in Hollywood to see an older, successful guy with a young blonde on his arm. Being a young blonde, I've had plenty of propositions, but I really wasn't into older men. I did, however, go out with two older guys. One was Mike Farrell (not the actor, but the music agent). He represented clients like Phil Collins and Julian Lennon. I dated him while I was also seeing a younger guy named Andy Hewitt, who worked for the big concert promoter Jim Nederlander.

Between Mike and Andy, I got around the music scene. I would have dinner with David Gilmour from Pink Floyd one night, then Phil Collins the next. We would squeeze in a drink with Rod Stewart on the weekend, then go to a vegetarian dinner with Annie Lennox. We had VIP tickets to all the concerts, living the "front row seats and backstage visiting" lifestyle. I am a singer myself and was in a pop rock band at the time, so I was really into it all.

One of my biggest thrills was meeting Julian Lennon right after his first record was released. Julian was in Los Angeles, and Mike and I went out to dinner with him and a few of his friends. Mike had to leave early for some reason, but told me to stay if I wanted. "Go on, have fun with them. Just take care of yourself."

After dinner we went back to Julian's suite at the Westwood Marquis and continued the party. Everyone was drinking champagne, and I was talking to Julian and listening to his tapes. Soon I noticed I was developing a major crush on him.

The next thing I knew, he asked me to stay the night. I was so nervous, I didn't know what to say. I wanted to stay, but I guess I was also worried that Mike would find out. It was really late so I told him that I had to call my mother. Can you believe that? I pretended to call her to see if it was okay. I hung up the phone and told Julian that I had to go home because my mother was upset that it was so late.

Now, in hindsight, I could kick myself for being so stupid. I told Julian that there would be another time and, of course, there was no other time. I never heard from him again. I guess I was the only girl to turn down Julian Lennon at the height of his career. What a claim to fame.

The other older man I dated besides Mike Farrell, the agent, was Jay Bernstein, the manager. He had "discovered" and guided the careers of Suzanne Somers, Farrah Fawcett, and many others. It started with Jay when my mother and I were having lunch at the Polo Lounge in the Beverly Hills Hotel. This pink hotel held a lot of great memories for me. When I was a kid my mother would take us on little weekend "vacations" at the hotel. We'd spend time by the pool, and I'd make friends with kids from all over who were on real vacations. We kids would run down the halls of the grand old place, ringing doorbells and then dashing off so as not to be caught by the guest in residence or worse, the manager. One time Elizabeth Taylor came to the door, and we ran screaming down the hall. That time we were caught and got in big trouble. But did we abandon the practice? Only long enough to let the heat cool off. Some kids did the toilet-paper thing in their neighborhoods for kicks. I rang bells at the Beverly Hills Hotel.

Anyhow, years later my mother and I were having lunch at the hotel, and we ran into Ed McMahon and Jay Bernstein. Jay knew my mother very well. He came over to our table and started fawning over me. "Oh my God, you've grown up," he said. After our lunch my mother had to get back to work, but Jay invited me to stay on for dessert with him and Ed McMahon.

Jay and Ed talked about how much they loved and admired my dad. At one point Jay started mimicking my father's voice, and it gave me chills. I was blown away. Jay is a very nice-looking man, so when he asked me if it was all right if he called me, I said sure, why not?

My interest in him was kind of a father thing. I was much more interested in hearing stories about my dad than in anything else Jay might have had in mind. He picked me up one night, and we went out to dinner. We had a lot to drink and talked and laughed. Before I knew it, he was asking me to marry him. "Let's go to Bora Bora and get married," he proposed.

We didn't go to Bora Bora to get married on our first date, but I did continue to go out with him. He used to send me the biggest arrangements of flowers in the city of Los Angeles. We'd have lovely dinners and get wasted on cocktails and then go home. I never had sex with Jay Bernstein, but he was a good flower-sender and dinner date. Though I think he really did want to get married, to me we just weren't soul mates. Unlike so many women in this town, I just couldn't get interested in older men.

HOLLYWOOD, 1985

My Roommate Heidi Fleiss, before She Was a Madam

I knew Heidi Fleiss way before she became the infamous Hollywood madam. We met at a club in L.A. one night, through Russell, a guy I dated briefly. Heidi was there with her best friend, Janie, whom she had known since grade school. Janie disliked me from the moment we met, but it was the opposite with Heidi and me. We clicked immediately.

Russell invited us all to have a few drinks, and we headed for Helena's, the in-crowd club that Jack Nicholson owned. Everyone seemed to have a great time that night. Afterward Heidi and I became new best friends. We were pretty inseparable for about four years. She was even at my side when I got engaged to a guy named Todd Mitchell.

After Todd came into the picture, the three of us hung out together constantly.

When we first met, Heidi was working as a waitress at Cravings restaurant on Sunset. One night we were invited to Bernie Cornfeld's house for a party. He used to have this huge estate and was always having blowout parties. Heidi didn't want to go, but I kind of forced her to come along with me and Todd.

When we got up to the house it was quite a scene. All kinds of celebrities were arriving for the party. Inside there was a buffet fit for a king, surrounded by elaborate ice sculptures. Soon the king himself, Bernie Cornfeld, walked over to us. I introduced him to Heidi, and the two of them fell head over heels for each other instantly. I spent the remainder of the evening alone with Todd. We had to practically pull Heidi out of that house. It was the beginning of her long relationship with Bernie.

Bernie owned Max Modeling Agency, and beautiful girls were always around him. Heidi would sit behind a desk and kind of help out at the agency. I think she wanted to keep her eye on Bernie. She'd also go on trips to Europe with Bernie, along with ten or twelve beautiful models.

After a while Heidi moved into Bernie's house. Things seemed to be going all right until one day she walked in on him having sex with another woman. She was so upset that she tried to kill herself, slitting her wrists. I saw her afterward and pleaded with her to stop hurting herself. "He's not worth it! He's not worth it," I said. She told me that she loved him so much, she didn't know what to do.

Things never got much better with Heidi and Bernie. He screwed everything that walked and still professed his love for her. She had a lot of trouble handling the situation and began to pull away from him, staying at her father's place more and more.

One time Heidi got her revenge on Bernie. There was a good-looking guy at a party in Heidi's father's condo. Heidi snuck off during the party and had sex with this guy for a couple of hours. Who should show up at the condo after Heidi left but Bernie, with his kid, and with food for everybody. After about an hour of waiting for Heidi, he was so mad that his face was turning purple. Finally she arrived—with hickeys all over her neck and face.

Bernie lost it. This man could not have been angrier if his head had been on fire. He yelled at Heidi, screaming about all he had done for her, about the car he gave her, the clothes, the house to live in, the opportunities, and this was how she repaid him! She just listened and didn't bother to mention her boyfriend's double standard of fidelity.

At that time my relationship with Todd was not that much better than Heidi's with Bernie. In some ways perhaps it was worse. Todd had a problem with drug and alcohol abuse that had led to violence several times. Once I ended up with a concussion. Todd and I broke up about the same time that Heidi and Bernie were breaking up. I needed to find a roommate and Heidi volunteered. We moved into a place on Doheny.

Todd and I kept getting back together, and he still came over to our apartment a lot, though I was really trying to break away from him. One time we had a fight, and he was raging. He grabbed me and held me upside down, threatening to drop me. He was a really big guy, and I was terrified he would break my neck. Heidi came running in and pleaded with him to stop. I think she brought him to his senses because he let me down gently.

Heidi was a very bright girl. She said she liked older men because the younger ones weren't smart enough for her. I'm not so sure she picked the best older men, however. Around the time she was breaking up with Bernie, she met

Ivan Nagy. That was the real beginning of the Heidi Fleiss story.

Ivan seemed to me to be a carbon copy of Bernie in many ways. For one thing, he wanted to screw all of Heidi's friends. I think I was one of the few he never came on to, probably because Heidi and I were roommates and very close. I also found myself in the middle of many of their fights. I believe I was the only person who could calm them down during their heated battles, although not always.

One night, while we were sleeping, Ivan vandalized Heidi's car. He called the next morning and told Heidi to go check out her car. We went downstairs and found her BMW completely trashed. The windshield had been busted and the body smashed in several places. Heidi seemed totally confused. "So we had a fight? Is this necessary?" she kept repeating. "I thought everything was okay."

I guess the car bashing sent Heidi packing, because she flew off to Europe with Bernie. Heidi was no sooner gone when Ivan called and invited me and Todd to lunch at the Hard Rock Cafe. "I know she doesn't want to be with Bernie," Ivan told us over the meal. "How can we get her back from Europe?" Ivan was crazy about Heidi. He cooked up all kinds of schemes to get her back. As I listened to Ivan, I realized that my friend Heidi was getting herself in even deeper between these two men, and it was going to be nothing but problems. Little did I know, of course, what real problems lay ahead for Heidi.

Sometimes Heidi was a great friend, and sometimes she wasn't. One night, before Todd and I finally broke up for good, he spent the night at our apartment. The next day I had a singing audition and left for a couple of hours. When I returned and walked into the bedroom, there was Todd, wearing only a little cropped T-shirt, with his pants nowhere in sight. He was lying on the floor, on his stomach, looking up at Heidi, who was talking on the phone. They were laughing and carrying on.

"What the fuck is this about?" I said. "What is going on here? Fuck you. Fuck you both," I screamed at them. Before either of them could respond, I stormed out and slammed the door. I didn't actually see anything except my naked-assed boyfriend. Heidi and Todd had always been like brother and sister, yet a few times she had told me how cute she thought he was. Who knows what they had been doing?

"Jenn, look," she later told me, "Todd was running around being stupid. Absolutely nothing happened, nothing at all. I don't see Todd that way." She convinced me that it was all innocent. Heidi was, after all, my best friend. Much later I learned from Todd that they had in fact fooled around a few times.

I never suspected that Heidi was into prostitution when we lived together. If she was, she kept it from me completely. A few times I did think it was strange that she was

flying to New York to meet men who would take her shopping for anything she wanted. But I was young, and frankly I didn't think much about it at the time.

On one of her trips Heidi met a girl on the plane who had been a Penthouse Pet. Her name was Mindy, and Heidi was really into her. One night she was over at the apartment, and the three of us shared a salad and watched television. It got late, and I went to bed. A couple of hours later Heidi knocked on my door and woke me up. She wanted to borrow my vibrator. It was just an old broken-down one that Todd had fixed. I still have it to this day. Heidi promised me that if she could use it she'd buy me a new one. She never did. I guess after the good time she and Mindy had with it, Heidi forgot.

Until that night, I hadn't realized that Heidi was bisexual. My own relationship with her never became sexual, however. The only time we ever touched in a very personal way was back when she was seeing Bernie Cornfeld. She was pregnant with his child and her nipples were really sore. She asked me to dab some cocaine on her nipples to numb them, so I did. Not long after that Heidi decided to have an abortion.

I never had a problem with Heidi's bisexuality, but at one point we did have a fight over drugs. Mindy was the instigator. At this point Mindy was dating Pauly Shore, who wasn't yet a star. Mindy and Pauly would hang out at our place high on coke. After my breakup with Todd, I had checked into a drug rehab to get off drugs myself. I certainly didn't want to start doing drugs again, so I made Heidi promise there wouldn't be any drugs in our apartment after I got home.

Not long after I returned, Mindy informed me that Heidi still had coke in the house. I was really angry and confronted Heidi. She was very cool about it all and actually flushed the coke down the toilet. Though she later had a series of drug problems, at that time she seemed to be able to sober up whenever she put her mind to it.

Besides Mindy, there were other women in Heidi's life. One was a girl named Bridget, whom Heidi seemed to truly love. Whether it was sexual or not, I don't know. One day Bridget decided to take an office job in a dangerous downtown neighborhood. Heidi pleaded with her not to take it but to no avail. Then the worst happened. A man came into the building where Bridget worked and raped and murdered her. Heidi was absolutely devastated. She became obsessed with finding Bridget's killer. She appeared on the television show *America's Most Wanted*, which actually helped the police catch the guy. Heidi wanted him to get the death penalty, but he got life. I believe Heidi is still in touch with Bridget's mother to this day.

Heidi was also friends and, I think, lovers with another girl, Linda, who had a serious drug problem. Heidi brought Linda home to our apartment to help her dry out. There was a lot of drama when Linda stayed with us, as there often is with drug addicts.

Linda had an ex-girlfriend, Antonia, a very skinny black girl who was after Linda and wanted her back on drugs. One night she found out that Linda was staying with us and showed up at our door. I told Antonia matter-of-factly that Linda didn't want to see her. But this gal wouldn't quit. I had to slam the door in her face. Then she pounded on the door and rang the bell, swearing at the top of her lungs.

I started yelling at her to "get out of here." Linda was crazed out of her mind at the prospect of seeing Antonia, and I was trying to protect her. Night after night Antonia kept coming back. We went through these screaming and yelling matches, but we never let her in.

Before I lived with Heidi I didn't realize that some people go on food binges when they are getting sober. Late at night, Linda would head across the street to buy several cooked chickens and down them all at one sitting. When the kitchen light woke me up, I'd join her at the table and watch in amazement. I've seen her polish off two birds and start working on a third. Not surprisingly, she began to put on weight. Heidi loved it. She would rub Linda's stomach and say, "Isn't that cute?" I didn't know it at the time, but I later learned that Linda was a prostitute.

The first news I had that Heidi was into prostitution was after she moved out of our apartment, around 1988. Heidi told me. We were driving in her black Corvette convertible one day, and she looked at me and said, "Someday, they'll be writing books about me, Jenn. They'll be making movies about me someday."

"What are you talking about?" I asked, puzzled.

"I'm a madam," she answered.

She had this smile on her face. I was shocked, but I told her that it was her life, her business, and I still loved her as a friend. I had met Heidi when I was just twenty-one and we had been friends for years. What do you do when your longtime friend tells you she's into prostitution?

NEW YORK, 1990

Off the Pages of a Romance Novel— Three Days with Grant Show

Shortly after I broke up with Todd for the last time, my mother, Elaine, was headed to New York to be on *Geraldo*. She'd been on his show a number of times, talking about everything from life in Hollywood to plastic surgery to my father. I was pretty miserable after my breakup with Todd and really needed to get out of town, so I went along with her. We traveled with her friend and right-hand man, Gregory Gibbs, and his lover, Vincent.

One night the four of us were having dinner at a Manhattan restaurant called Columbus. Soon after we arrived I noticed this really cute guy. I think Gregory and Vincent might have actually spotted him first, but we all agreed he was drop-dead gorgeous. My mother said to me, "You know what? I want to fix you up with him, Jennifer."

"You're kidding," I said. "He's got to be waiting for some girl to join him." Gregory thought he looked married, but Vincent was screaming at me to "go for it!"

Mom said I was too negative and suggested that we introduce ourselves to him. She was trying hard to get me to forget about Todd. While I was still pondering the issue, Vince got up from the table and walked over to him. Vince learned that he was waiting for someone who apparently had stood him up. Vince brought him over to meet us.

It turned out that this gorgeous guy was an actor on the soap opera *Ryan's Hope*. His name was Grant Show, now famous for *Melrose Place* but then known only to daytime-soap fans. Grant stayed with us for dinner, and he and I hit it off quite well. "Why don't you meet me over at the China

Club tonight?" he suggested as we were leaving. "Okay, great, I'll see you there," I said, really excited to get the invitation.

Mom had to be at the studio early the next morning so she excused herself and went back to our shared hotel room. "Don't stay out too late," she warned me in a motherly fashion as Gregory and Vincent and I headed off to the China Club. Once we were inside the club, we ran into Grant almost instantly. He grabbed my hand and said, "Come on, let's dance."

I was totally flipped out. There were so many good-looking men in the club that I thought I had died and gone to dating heaven. But there were also plenty of beautiful women. The next thing I knew, my handsome New Yorker spotted a tall, gorgeous blonde. He took my hand and led me over to her. As they talked I was certain that I was history with him. She was so beautiful that I figured I didn't have a chance. But then he pulled me back onto the dance floor again.

We danced, had a few drinks, and really enjoyed the night together. We left the club and went to a bar for another drink. I was drinking cranberry juice, but he seemed able to handle the hard stuff, even though he had to be on the set at 7 A.M. the next morning. He took me back to my hotel and walked me into the lobby. We stood there looking at one another. Then he kissed me, and I started to melt.

"Do you want to get a room?" he asked me. At this point I had not been with anyone but Todd for something like four and a half years. I thought to myself, "If this is going to be a one-night stand, then so be it, I'm okay with that."

"Yes, I want to get a room," I told this gorgeous creature.

We walked to the registration desk. The girl behind the

counter was about twenty years old. She recognized Grant and started gushing, "Oh my God, you're . . . oh my God, it's you!" She used his character's name on the soap. I had never seen his show and didn't have a clue what she was carrying on about. All I knew was that I was going up to a room with him, and she wasn't.

We got into our room and, of course, we had sex. He was the most romantic lover I'd ever had or imagined in my entire life. We made love for hours, until daylight came and we had to stop so he could get to the set.

He gave me his number since I was going to be in New York for a couple more days. I was surprised because I thought I would never see him again. He left for the studio and I went to sleep, getting up in time to join my mother and a friend of hers for lunch at Le Cirque.

Mom was dating some big shot at Revlon at the time, and we were supposed to have dinner with him that night. When we got back to the hotel I called my mom's friend and asked if I could bring a date for the evening. He said fine, so I called my soap opera lover and asked him to dinner. He called me right back and said he would love to see me again. I was really excited.

My mom's friend sent a limo over to Grant's place to get him, since the rest of us were already at the restaurant and Grant was running late. I was sure that Grant had changed his mind and wasn't coming. But he did appear. He walked down the long hall of the restaurant, his jacket over his shoulder and his hair slicked back. I couldn't believe how gorgeous he was.

He sat down next to me. All throughout dinner Grant and I touched each other under the table. We couldn't wait to go back to his place. When we finally got there, he lit a hundred candles all over the apartment. We drank chilled wine, and he put on some romantic music.

As Sam Cooke's "You Send Me" played, he told me how beautiful I was. "It's got to be a line," I thought, "but here he is, spending another night with me." If it was just a one-night stand I would not be in his apartment surrounded by candles and wine and romantic music. We went into his bedroom and had sex, incredible sex that lasted three or four hours. He was dripping sweat from our love-making exertion. Best of all, he had a slightly curved private part that hit me perfectly in just the right spot. I've never had a better lover in my life than Grant Show. The way he held me and the way he looked at me made me feel so wanted and so loved. He told me that I was beautiful every other minute while we were in bed, and his kisses were passionate and deep. Grant Show was the perfect lover, a role-model lover to fulfill every woman's romantic fantasy. I didn't care who he was or what he did.

The next morning we went to Soho for breakfast with my mom. Then we went shopping, and he bought me an expensive pair of tights. I still have them to this day.

Our last day together ended, and I had to catch my plane. We exchanged numbers, but our lives went their own ways. I soon left for Japan to sing, and he was busy building his acting career. We eventually lost touch.

Athough it turned out to be just a three-day affair with Grant, those were three days I'll never forget. Looking back I can't help but think of him as a character off the pages of a perfect romance novel. I do get to see him every week on *Melrose Place*—and you can bet that I watch the show. Recently, Grant was on the cover of *TV Guide*, and I was looking at it in the presence of my then-boyfriend. "You're in love with that guy," my boyfriend said, looking at my expression. I ended up saying simply, "It was a long time ago." Grant is in love with Laura Leighton now. All I can say is that she is one lucky woman.

BEVERLY HILLS, 1992

Waiting for Stallone

*B*y now I was certainly over Todd, dating a new guy and, of course, keeping up with the L.A. party scene. One night a girlfriend and I were at the nightclub Spice. Sylvester Stallone was at the club with several friends. We hung around Sly's group and had a great time. As we were leaving and getting into my mom's Jag convertible, which I had borrowed for the night, a guy from Sly's entourage came over to us and said, "Hey, do you girls want to come up to Sly's house for a little party?"

We were game. We followed the guy in his black Lexus up Benedict Canyon to Stallone's really gorgeous house. By the time we arrived, the party was already under way. The late comic Sam Kinnison was there telling jokes, and the drinks were flowing.

The relationship I was involved in then was pretty obsessive. When we arrived at the party, I wanted to call my boyfriend and tell him I would come over to his place afterward. While I was looking for the phone, a man started following me around, coming on to me and telling me how much he wanted to be with me. Meanwhile, this man's girlfriend, who was also at the party, was watching him. She came over to me and started letting me have it for seducing her man. "Wait a minute," I screamed at her, "I'm not doing anything. He's the jerk who's coming on to me! Don't blame me. I'm just looking for a phone."

I escaped from that nightmare and found a phone. While I was talking to my boyfriend, Sylvester Stallone came over to me and whispered, "I hope you're not talking long-distance to Cuba." Not wanting to worry him, I got off the phone and tried to find a bathroom.

I couldn't find a bathroom anywhere in this major house. First, I walked into Sly's bedroom. A girl was there, sitting on the bed, wearing sexy lingerie. "Oh hi, I said. "Sorry to interrupt you. I was just looking for a bathroom." The girl replied, "No problem. I'm just waiting for Sly." I left and kept searching for a bathroom.

The next stop was the kitchen, where I found a pretty girl sitting at a table. "Do you know where the bathroom is?" I asked. "No, I don't know," she said. "I've never been here before. I'm just waiting for Sly." So I left the kitchen and tried a bunch of other doors.

I wandered into the screening room. Sitting in the dark room was another girl. "Do you know where the restroom is?" It was my standard line. My search had turned into an expedition for lost treasure in the House of Sly. Guess what she answered? That's right. "No, I'm just waiting for Sly."

This was all too funny. One, two, three, maybe an entire house full of girls were sitting in different rooms waiting for Sly. I still couldn't find a bathroom, but I found out what goes on around the Stallone house. I also figured out why the guy in the black Lexus asked me and my girlfriend to come to the party. I'm sure it was to fill up more rooms in this huge house with choices for old Sly.

I finally found a bathroom and rushed in. By now I really had to use it. The second I was inside there was a banging on the door. I shouted to the intruder to wait a minute. I finished my business and opened the door. Standing there was the same guy who had been following me around earlier. He rushed past me, shut the bathroom door behind him, and was all over me. "You're so beautiful. You're so sexy. You're so desirable. All I want is you."

"You're full of you know what," I shouted as I pushed him away. "Your girlfriend is here. She's already hassling me, and I'm not interested in you!" I managed to get by him and out of the bathroom.

After that narrow escape, I found another phone because I had to call my boyfriend back. The minute I dialed the phone Sly walked in and said, "You're sure that you're not calling Cuba? What's going on? Why are you on my phone?"

All I could think was, "You cheap son of a bitch, what do you care if I'm calling the moon? Why don't you go and pick one of the women who are waiting for you all over the house instead of hassling me?" I guess he thought that I should have been waiting in one of the rooms, too. Only I don't wait for anybody. I was talking to my boyfriend and decided to keep on talking to him.

After a few hours the party began to wind down. Then Sly called it to an abrupt halt. He announced that everyone had to leave and leave right now. Party's over, scram, get lost now. Everyone filed out like it was a fire drill.

Sam Kinnison grabbed a bottle of Dom Perignon and a bottle of Cristal on his way out. "Take the champagne, just get out of here," shouted Stallone. I walked over to Sly to say good-bye and he said, "You know, you're kind of cute. Too bad you were on the phone the whole night. We might have gotten something going."

Here was this man with a house full of women waiting for him in every room and he still thought I believed that I might have been his choice for the night. Wow, how lucky can one girl get? I thanked him for the wonderful party and left to go spend the night with my boyfriend in Cuba.

LOS ANGELES, 1996

A Daring Proposal from Rob Camilletti

I first went out with Rob Camilletti, Cher's ex-boyfriend, in 1991. He had been on-again, off-again with Cher, and I ended up with him during an off-again period. We split up, and years later I ran into him again. We talked a couple of times, and I decided to show up one night at Bar One on Sunset, where Rob was the bartender. It was great seeing him again. He was flirting with me, and I was really into him. I knew I wanted him to come home with me that night. My roommate Diane was also with me at the club, and we were both talking to Rob.

At one point he whispered to me, "You know, it would be really kind of cool if your roommate watched us." Believe it or not, I'm shy and kind of old-fashioned when it comes to sex. I thought this was the most daring proposal I had ever heard in my life. "But, hey," I thought, "I really do want to be with him tonight."

A few minutes later Diane and I went into the ladies' room. I practically died of embarrassment when I asked her if she would watch me and Rob have sex. Diane started laughing. She thought Rob Camilletti was the hottest hunk in town and harbored a longtime crush on him. When she started talking about how cute his little ass was, I quickly interrupted her. "Look, here's the deal. I don't know if I can actually go through with this, but I'm going to try. It's what he wants, and I want him. So, you come into the room for like two minutes, then get out of the room, okay?" Diane agreed to the terms. I went back to Rob at the bar and told him we were on. Then Diane and I hung out and danced until the bar closed.

When we got back to my place, I was really nervous. I

had never done anything like this before. Rob showed up, and in what seemed like a second he and I had taken off all of our clothes and were having sex. Diane walked into the room. I immediately felt uncomfortable. Two minutes went by, then five, then fifteen minutes, and I thought, "What happened to our two-minute deal?"

After twenty minutes passed, I got up to go to the bath-room, followed by Diane. "What the hell are you doing?" I said to her. "We agreed on two minutes, not a lifetime!" I asked her not to return to the bedroom—enough is enough. She shrugged, "Rob has such a great ass. I love watching it go up and down."

Diane left us alone as promised and Rob and I finished having sex. Rob told me he didn't want to do it with Diane or any other girl. He just got off on having another woman watch. "I don't want to be with them," he would say. "I just want to be with you."

I liked him so much that we did it again with another girl watching, a Swedish friend of mine named Annika. On that occasion Rob and I were having sex on the floor of my living room, and Annika was in the other room. Rob called out to her to come in and watch. She came in, and he started talking to her while he was doing me. Then, to make it even worse, he told Annika to come closer, to sit on the side of the couch, right next to where we were having sex.

I have never participated in a *ménage* and have never been with another woman. This watching thing was the most daring sexual exploit I had ever done. I didn't particu-larly like it, but it sure got this man off.

After Annika I told Rob that I didn't want to do that anymore. We had sex a couple more times without a gal-lery, and he said to me, "See, it doesn't have to be the other way." I felt like saying, "What did Cher do when you brought in a crowd?" I do remember Cher on the talk shows when she was hot and heavy with Rob, telling the world that he was the best lover she had ever had in her life. I wondered what she meant. I also wondered why I had been so into Rob. I have always admired Cher so much. I think she is one of the most talented female performers in the world. Deep down I'm sure that the fact that he had been with Cher was part of my attraction to him. But it wasn't strong enough for me to continue having sex as a spectator sport.

Trouble in Tinseltown—Date Rape and Battering

Maybe it's the excesses of this town or maybe violence against women happens as much everywhere. I don't know. I only know that I've had my share of violent episodes with men.

Not long after I was out of high school, I went on a blind date that was set up through a friend. The guy took me to dinner and afterward we went back to his place. He kept pouring me drinks. Perhaps I should have known what he was doing, but I was so young. He started kissing me and then kept going further. I asked him to stop, but he didn't. Even though I was very high, I knew I didn't want to have sex with him, and I told him so. I kept saying no. He ignored me and kept on in a rough way until he forced himself on me. That was the only time I've ever actually been raped.

I left there crying, upset, and angry. I had the dirtiest

feeling in my gut. I didn't do anything about it then. Today I would. I still see him around town sometimes. And even though I have dealt with what he did to me, when I see him I still feel the emotions I felt then.

My first long-term relationship out of high school, with Todd, had moments of violence. But the most abusive relationship I've ever been a part of was with a guy named John from Tampa, Florida.

One Halloween night John and I and Heidi Fleiss all went to a party at Bar One. John was pretty drunk and at one point got upset with me because I told a girl he was talking to that I was his girlfriend. The next thing I knew he slammed my head against the bar. This huge lump started to swell up on my head. Heidi felt the lump and told John to take me home.

Once John and I were in the car heading home, it got worse. We were arguing, and he punched me in the head so hard that it cut my face right above the eye. Blood gushed everywhere. It scared him so much that he took me home and tried to take care of me. The next day I had to go to the hospital to get it sewn up. My face is still scarred from the cut.

When Heidi was with Ivan, I saw her with a black eye. I couldn't understand why, if he hit her, she would stay with him. Then, not long afterward, I got myself into the same kind of relationship. Now I understand those obsessive, violent relationships, and I'll never again let myself stay in one again. I learned about physical abuse the same way I learned about date rape—the hard way.

Navigating the Hollywood Fast Lane

I live in the Hollywood fast lane. I may not be a star yet, but I've been surrounded by famous people all my life. I grew up with them. People say a lot of negative things about Hollywood. And, even though it's my hometown, I can't deny most of what is said. There are many dishonest people here trying to make a buck any way they can, cashing in on the Hollywood myth, taking advantage of naive people with dreams of fame and riches. But there are also plenty of good folks here. It's just not always easy to find them.

Women, in particular, are definitely taken advantage of in Hollywood. A woman has to be especially strong-minded and strong-willed to make it here, to focus on what she wants to accomplish, and to be willing to work extra hard to get ahead. I have a head start here because of who my parents are. But it's still tough. And if you're a woman coming to Hollywood from a small town without connections, it is really, really difficult. It's easy to end up in the wrong hands. Too many beautiful girls listen to men who promise to put them into films. The next thing they know, the men are trying to get them into bed.

There's always the exception, however. Sissy Spacek is a good example of a woman with enormous talent who came to Hollywood without connections and eventually made it. Her friend Gus Savalas offered her money to go back home, and she turned him down, telling him, "I came out here to be a star and I will be a star." She wanted to be an actress, and she did it. Sissy is one of my favorite actresses, and her example is an inspiration.

For every Sissy Spacek, however, there are thousands

who get off on the wrong track. Tinseltown can eat pretty, naive, and ambitious young girls alive and spit them out. To some degree that has even happened to me, and I was prepared for what this town dishes out. Many young women who come here may have the talent to make it. The ones who meet with success are those who take their dreams seriously. They go to acting classes. They study singing and dancing, and they try to get legitimate work. To support themselves they work as waitresses or do whatever they can to pay the rent, without turning to prostitution.

I know some of the girls who worked for Heidi. Perhaps a few have gone on to straight jobs, but most have had a hard time getting out of that life. I don't understand it myself. Even though I've had my bouts with drugs and at times have been heavily into the party scene, I've never slept with a man for money. Even if I was so broke I felt I had to do it, I wouldn't. If I needed the money that badly, I'd get a job first, any kind of a job.

Looking back, I realize that I've been through a lot in my short life. I guess time moves faster in the fast lane. I've had many failed relationships. I have experienced drug and alcohol abuse, both my own and that of people I loved. I've had my share of career disappointments. I've gotten through it all with the help of a mother who loves me unconditionally. Elaine Young is one hell of a lady and one terrific mother. We're inseparable best friends today. I love her more than anything and believe that, with her love and support, life will turn out just fine.

I'm completely focused now on my singing and acting careers. People ask me if I want to follow in my father's footsteps. I do. I love my music and am now working on a single. And I also love acting—particularly improvisational acting. I realize that I'm not getting any younger, but I am getting better, stronger, and smarter. I spent too many years trying to please the men in my life. Now I'm concentrating on my own goals. If a man comes along who can be loving and supportive, that's fine, but that's not what I'm putting my efforts into.

I still think about my father every day, wishing for a few minutes with him, always wanting to know more about him. His last agent, Marty Baum, has possession of my father's Oscar statuette. I have so little that belongs to him and, as his only daughter, I feel I should have it. But, in what is perhaps typical of this town, I have to file a lawsuit to get to my father's Oscar. For me that Oscar is a symbol of what was wonderful and special about my father—his great talent. I know I have his talent in my genes, but I also have inherited some of his tendency toward self-destruction. I, too, have wasted years of my life on my addictions—drugs, parties, and men.

This book has given me a chance to reflect on that past and to resolve anew that the future will be brighter. It's also given me a chance to let people know that growing up with and hanging out with celebrities is not such a bed of roses. There's a great deal of excitement in it, but eventually you have to go back to your life, to you. If you don't know who you are and what you want, then who you know doesn't mean much.

So many of my fellow celebrity-kid friends have spent years being as lost and confused as I was. We've learned the hard way—that there's a lot in life more important than being seen with the latest hunk or hanging out at the hippest clubs. Now I know that, and the future for me looks a lot more hopeful than the past.